The Real Cost

By the same author

The Little Green Book: An Owner's Guide to the Planet
  with Richard Boston and Richard Holme
The Animals Report
Wild Britain
Working the Land, with Charlie Pye-Smith

THE REAL COST

Richard North

Chatto & Windus London

First published in 1986
by Chatto & Windus Ltd
40 William IV Street
London WC2N 4DF

British Library Cataloguing in Publication Data

North, Richard
   The Real Cost.
   1. Industry – Environmental aspects – Great
   Britain
   2. Great Britain – Industries
   I. Title
   304.2'8'0941   TD186.5.G7

   ISBN 0 7011 2729 5

Printed in Great Britain by
Butler & Tanner Ltd,
Frome, Somerset

4

Contents

For my parents

Acknowledgements

MY thanks go especially to Annie, my wife, who endured the longish haul that writing this book involved. My children, Polly, Matthew and Emma were pretty darned patient, too: they have never known other than an absentee father, who is too often incarcerated with the word processor.

Thanks are due to Philips for the continued loan of my beloved P2000, which has sped this process along. I am also grateful to Pete Mitchell who came and mended it with excellent dispatch and flair.

Mr H. Jackson, at the National Westminster Bank, went on lending me money when others would not have. I am, naturally, extremely indebted to him.

Frank Ellis, of the University of East Anglia, deserves my thanks, for having researched the way peasants get paid for their crops, and for a helpful conversation.

Charlie Pye-Smith was an unfailing friend and confidant, as well as an invaluable travelling companion during an unforgettable few weeks in Egypt.

We are grateful to the following for permission to reproduce the photographs: Earthscan, page 123; Impact Photos/Christopher Cormack, pages 26, 35, 88; Link/Orde Eliason for pages 19, 21, 53, 68, 74, 78, 93, 153, 162, 189; NHPA for pages 41, 43, 49, 51, 65, 99, 113, 120, 131, 183; World Wildlife Fund for pages 17, 144, 184. We should also like to acknowledge the following organisations, as well as some of the books mentioned in the Reading List, as sources for figures throughout the book: Earthscan; the Food and Agriculture Organisation of the United Nations; Oxfam; the Stockholm International Peace Research Institute; Worldwatch Institute, Washington DC.

Foreword

by David McTaggart, chairman of Greenpeace International

DURING the last twenty years or so there has been a gradual, inexorable, if somewhat painful growth in public awareness of the fragility and delicacy of the environment. Within the last ten years, this awareness has reached new heights. Even the major political parties, bludgeoned into activity by public opinion, are openly concerned about the influence of the 'Greens' and have gone to the unprecedented lengths of drafting environmental policy papers to head off the growing threat through the ballot box.

Now, as much through necessity as through choice, ordinary people and political parties alike are required to grapple with the problems of how to reconcile the desire for growth and prosperity with the constraints imposed by a finite world. This revision of thought is putting the basis upon which manufacturing and consumer economies are founded under increasing scrutiny. The inequalities of a world which allows excess for some and abject poverty for the many are compounded and underlined by the realisation of the inadequacies of traditional growth policies and of the materialism which necessarily accompanies them.

We are experiencing the first faltering steps towards recognising a fundamental and unpalatable truth: for too long the environment, human and physical resources and, most of all, human wisdom have been sacrificed on the altar of growth. A wind of change is at last blowing. Every action we take, every article we manufacture, every 'development' we approve has a range of effects and consequences which go far beyond those we immediately perceive. Whether it be the clearing of forests in Brazil or the use of uranium in reactors or even the manufacturing of the humble plastic container, the effects must be gauged not only as pluses and minuses for jobs and the creation of wealth, but also for the health and viability of the environment as a whole.

Richard North's book opens yet another door on this vital debate. It explains with clarity and directness the true cost imposed on this fragile planet by the actions of society.

Change must come; it is an inevitability. Growth for growth's sake is untenable and unsustainable. The Earth has only so much to offer. If society does not come to terms with the finite nature of the resources upon which many of its economies are based, the result will undoubtedly be social dislocation on a global scale. To minimise the value of resources by producing goods which are superfluous to human needs and which are designed to become obsolete in the shortest possible time contradicts the most basic of economic principles. Either we change now, by choice, or we change later through necessity and suffer the consequences.

To make any decision, we need information. Richard North's book gives us the tools with which we can begin to construct a more sustainable world. It lays down a challenge to our decision-makers which they ignore at their – and our – peril. Every reader of this book can and must use it as a stimulus to inspire individual action in our daily lives and corporate action through our elected representatives.

Introduction

'The lowest real commodity prices since the 1930s, the sharp slowdown in world trade in the early 1980s, and the contraction of industrial countries' demand for Third World imports caused by restrictive monetary and fiscal policies (in varying combinations) have all contributed to developing countries' problems.'
Michael Prest, *The Times*, 20 Sept 1985

I would like this book to play a part in making people feel that this world is, in its fabulous diversity, an extraordinary skein of interconnections and dependencies. It might have been subtitled An Ecology of Modern Man. Ecology teases out the connections between life systems and the world in which they exist. I am nourished because of the work of Brazilian cattle men in one-time forest land. This book goes some way to sketching out how that happens, and with what consequences.

The tea-pickers of Bangladesh, for instance, are a long way away from those of us in the West, but their hands put the tea in front of us as surely as the hand that put the kettle on or stacked the packets on the shelf of our local supermarket. I want to emphasise that our *pleasure* in the produce of a more equitable world would be far greater than in our present distorted one, where rich consumers buy the produce of poor people too cheaply (or see the money they pay side tracked into the pockets of middlemen who ill deserve it).

I have found few people to characterise as monsters. The multinationals, a favourite target, are not always angels, but their acts are often caused by the consumers who want their products to be cheap. Besides, multinationals are more open to persuasion and the consciences of consumers than the many, very distant, small-time entrepreneurs who abuse their own locals far more cruelly. Aid agencies and governments have taken a long time to realise that small-time, property-owning peasants are highly productive and deserve encouragement. That kind of localised capitalism was not much favoured by the first wave of post-colonialists who thought about development and favoured the economies of large-scale production.

One major factor has not been much discussed in the book. This is the

9

horrendous national debts of many Third World countries. At the end of 1984, developing countries owed around $470 billion of outstanding foreign debt. There is a crisis of confidence about the ability of poorer countries, especially in Latin America, to pay interest on their loans. In the heady years after the mid-1970s oil price hike, when oil exporting countries flooded the banks with surplus capital, poor countries were encouraged in extravagant borrowing, often for large-scale schemes which have proved useless or worse. The poor countries of the world have now accumulated debt equivalent to $100 for every man, woman, or child on earth: many of them are forced to grow crops which feed the rich world, in order to pay debts incurred on disastrous agricultural schemes which failed to feed their indigenous hungry.

The years of surplus have long gone. World recession, a collapse of confidence, high interest rates and a strong dollar have all made rich countries wary of lending to poor ones, and rendered poor ones much less capable of repaying their existing debts. Many of them have had their debts 'rescheduled' (deferred, or extended, or made repayable at reduced interest). Debts were one of many factors which have forced a dramatic reduction in per capita living standards in many poor countries. But the story is enormously complex and the crude statistics disguise the facts as much as reveal them. The situation is very unpredictable, with major diplomatic moves likely to forestall some of the difficulties. They are immense – many poor countries now use over a third of all their export earnings simply in paying debts.

This book does not take an overview. Instead, it tries, case by case, to pencil in some lines of connection and dependency. I am afraid you will look in vain here for a Judgement Day account of what it all adds up to and where it's all going. It is hard enough to stay on top of the mountain of information (a mountain which is, none the less, a molehill compared to what would have been needed for this book to be definitive), without pretending to usurp the role of celestial accountant.

This is not a doomsday book. I have no idea whether the world will be, in overall terms, a better or worse place 20 or 100 years from now. And if most of us do better, that will hardly soothe the misery of those who do worse. I do not suppose that peanut production or cattle grazing on fragile land will see off mankind, though they are clearly inappropriate. I do not even suppose that nuclear power stations are inherently worse than their acid-rain producing, coal-fired cousins. The world is a very big curate's egg: good, and bad, in parts. It is also very complicated, very diverse. Even in the midst of tragedy there are good signs. For instance, by September 1985 there was news that the rains in large parts of Africa were back to normal. For some regions at least, progress could be made after appalling suffering.

I understand absolutely the urge of man to sit down, with his computers and research papers, and try to work out whether he is doing well or badly in his management of this planet. Unfortunately, his urge to be encyclopaedic, to take an overview or to generalise, has led to two very conflicting sorts of work and view, neither of which holds a monopoly on the truth. In a nutshell, we have people now divided into Doom or Boom merchants. *The Limits to Growth*, published in the early 1970s, (see **Reading List**) had computer projections of finite resources: The argument turned out to be very flawed, being unable to take proper account of an uncertain future and especially of our ability to foresee, and duck, crises, or imaginatively to invent our way out of them.

There was, in 1980, *Global 2000* (see **Reading List**), a brave attempt by President Carter and his environmentalists to look at the pressures population and production would put on the world. What could be more responsible in the leader of a powerful nation dedicated to economic growth than to wonder if we were not behaving like children: having fun, but not clearing up our mess after us? Another Doom piece.

Then the late Herman Kahn and his associates delivered, in 1984, *The Resourceful Earth* (see **Reading List**), which pointed out that *Global 2000* avoided the good news and made the classic mistake of projecting the future from the present, as though man did not learn as he lived and struggled. The future is not the day before yesterday and today projected forward. It grows, surely enough, from the past, but with new events and factors moulding and creating what will be obvious to those who live it, but is unknown to us who are going to be its parents and grandparents.

But *The Resourceful Earth*, for all its gung-ho faith in the market and human ingenuity, did at least admit that it was evidence of mistakes and problems which made men seek new alternatives. If we clean up our smokestacks and lakes, it is because whistle-blowers unfashionably point out the value of clear skies and fresh water. The merchants of Boom need to be checked by the disciples of Doom. The Boom people give us the products and services we all enjoy, too many of them for our own good, but even then at our behest. The Doom people remind us to think about both the real, often small, value of what we consume, and the often large damage which flows from that consumption.

The Real Cost seldom attempts to present a global picture. But I have picked some subjects which have little to do with either rich-world consumption or direct purchase by richer countries. Indeed, in **Birth** I have tried to discuss some of the opportunities and hazards facing the new small persons arriving in the world, and facing all of us as a result of their arrival. It is the chapter which you might consider using as your starting point.

1 Births: opportunities and problems

During the first 300,000 years of Man's existence, 46 billion members of the species Homo sapiens have inhabited the earth. Thus, a neat 10% of the total number of Homo sapiens that have ever lived are alive now. In 1982, 77.5 million more people were alive on this planet than in 1981.

Their fates will be very varied, ranging from the classic indices of technological development to the primitively vital. But the pictures are not uniform. There are rich people in poor countries and poor people in rich countries. In the US, for instance, 20 million people, a quarter of them children, spent a hungry 1984, and in the south west of the US there is considerable incidence of hunger-related diseases more commonly seen in the Third World.

Though babies in the poor world have an average 50% 70% greater chance of living to see their first birthday than was accorded them 20 years ago, it remains 10 times more likely that they will die in their first year of life than will a baby in the rich world. That they will get to their fourth birthday is 10 times more likely for the rich world baby than for the Third World baby. In the Gambia, Sierra Leone and Malawi, 1 baby in 5 does not live a year, in spite of improvements in infant survival in those countries.

For decades there has been a torrent of predictions about world population. Suggestions that it will grow hugely have failed to take into account the way in which the world's food production is so little managed for equitability and ecological sustainability. In many places mass starvation will in the future be a bitter limiter of population growth.

However, though the rise in populations is large and many poor citizenries are expected to double by the end of the century – especially in countries ill-equipped to feed or provide sanitation for their people – there are many signs that countries can limit growth quite effectively by social control, encouragement, or by perhaps the most effective and least degrading means: education.

Unfortunately, increases of population are cumulative. Thus, though there may appear to be little difference between a 1%, 2% or 3% growth rate in a population, in a single century they account for a 270%, 724% and 1922%

"In 1984 the world's population will increase by about 80 million. Most of the increase, about 73 million, will occur in developing countries, now comprising about three-quarters of world population."

World Development Report **World Bank, July 1984**

Date	Historical period	Population
298,000 BC	Origin of Homo Sapiens	2 millions
40,000 BC	Early Stone Age — man the wanderer	3 million
8,000 BC	From hunter to farmer — man settles down	5 million
0	Start of the Christian era (actually 1 AD)	200 million
1650	The age of learning	500 million
1830	The beginnings of industrialisation	1,000 million (1 billion)
1945	The nuclear age takes shape	2,300 million
1986	The present	4,600 million

growth in *numbers* respectively. In most cases, it is only when the population is stable or falling that a poor nation can make progress in feeding its people. However, in order to stabilise self-sufficiency in the Third World, massive reforms in international agricultural practices would be required.

The scale of the problem is evident. Nigeria has less than a third of the population of Russia, but must each year attempt to feed 2.8 million more mouths, whilst Russia's growth in numbers is rather lower, at 2.2 million. China's and India's populations grow dramatically every year: 15% and 13% respectively.

In Europe, however, many countries now have stable populations, and whilst China's policies for birth control are a draconian mixture of incentives and penalties (with enforced sterilisation more common than is often admitted, and the continuation of infanticide of female babies far from unknown), they have managed a decline in births per thousand people of nearly a third. Even so, with a population growth of more than 1%, it will be a phenomenal task to hold China's population to 1200 million (as against the current 1008 million) by the end of the century.

Whilst bribes of various sorts have brought forward people to volunteer for sterilisation in India and Bangladesh, in some states, notably Kerala in southern India, unusually low fertility rates have been achieved by women – uncommonly well educated there – opting for birth control.

Only a third of women in developing countries use contraceptives, as against 72% in developed countries, although nearly half the women in various Third World surveys have said they do not want any more babies. In the Third World, women with schooling do have fewer babies on average – generally speaking, 2 or 3 children fewer – while women in Bangladesh with

"Africa's 10 richest countries have virtually the same population growth rates as the 10 poorest."

New Scientist
9 August 1984

7 or more years schooling are 5 times as likely to use contraceptives as their less educated sisters.

The affordability of contraceptives may pose a problem to women in poorer countries who often, in any event, feel the need to have families large enough to provide economic support for them in their old age. Part of the difficulty of considering fertility rates is that the merits of a stable or declining birth rate in a community (if they exist at all, which is disputed) are social. If *everyone* reduces the size of their family, there is more to go round; if only one family does, against the trend, there are fewer children to help the parents in their old age when they will have to fight the very shortages which the extra births have generated. This is a good example of the 'tragedy of the commons' concept, in which *everyone* must do the right thing for there to be a chance of an advantage to the individual in doing so.

What is there for each of us?

There are about 1.5 billion hectares of cropland in the world and more than 3 billion hectares of pasture land. There are also about 4 billion hectares of forest and woodland. Over 8 billion hectares of land are therefore capable of being productive to some degree: about 2 hectares per person.

Arthur Westing, one of our most original ecologists, decided to analyse the world in terms of what its carrying capacity might be, at various living standards, given current agricultural production.

The important questions are these: with present agricultural production, what level of population, worldwide, could be sustained at affluent levels of consumption (roughly those that obtain in the rich nations – at least twice the world average gross national product per capita) and what numbers could be supported assuming austere living standards (roughly those obtaining in nations with between half and twice the present GNP)?

Arthur Westing reckoned that world population would have to be at least halved if an affluent standard were to be achievable and made general; an austere standard of living could be provided for anything between three quarters and two thirds of the present population. By one calculation, a quarter of the present world population could be given a US standard of living.

However, beyond the political revolution or reformation that would be required to make distribution of the world's huge wealth more equitable, there are other severe problems. For example, land reform will be needed in many countries if peasants are to grow food for themselves and their neighbours rather than for rich nations (see **Coffee, Tea, Sugar** and **Bananas**). The greatest difficulty is likely to be encountered in the politics of poor countries, where sustainable farming to feed people may well not be to the taste and interests of the powerful sections of the community.

It now looks as though the vast progress that has been made in wringing from the soils of the earth some sort of a living for her growing numbers is coming to an end, at least temporarily. Much of the increase in production has taken place at the cost of ecologically sustainable farming techniques (see **Irrigation**), and in the rich world involves, crucially, vast inputs of fossil fuels (see **Livestock** and **Milk**), which are themselves non-renewable. We are therefore mining our food, more than growing it. Between the Second World War and now, the per capita amount of cropland in the world fell by one third, but the fertiliser use per capita multiplied by 5. To take cereals as an example, the fastest growth in supplies took place between the Second World War and 1973: an annual 3% increase, or a doubling across the period. But the world's farmers are now achieving barely 2% growth, while successive droughts in Africa have been hitting the poorest hardest.

Soil loss

The soil in which the world grows its food is disappearing at an alarming rate. Spurred on by cheap fertilisers, Western farmers have abandoned fallow periods and crop rotation on their land, thus encouraging soil and fertility loss (although they do make up some of the deficit in chemical inputs).

Hungry poor-world farmers have started pressing steeper and steeper slopes into service (usually without the terrace-work which their forebears used to keep soils in place), and have also abandoned fallow periods and crop rotation in an attempt to keep production high, at least in the short term, which is all they can afford to think about (see **Peanuts** and **Cooking**). Africa and Asia may lose between them almost 1 billion tonnes of soil to the wind annually – the soil blows out over the oceans in great plumes which can be clearly seen from satellites.

The Yellow and Ganges rivers between them cart around 3 billion tonnes of soil a year away from their watersheds. In India it is reckoned that the annual harvest robs soils of around 18.5 million tonnes of nutrients, but that little more than 10 million tonnes (half of it organic waste and half chemical fertiliers) is replaced. This sizeable 'fertility gap' bodes ill for that country's need to take food production from the present 130 million tonnes of food grains to nearer 240 million if it is to feed a population reckoned to be in the region of a billion by the turn of the century (the population is about 680 million now).

About a half of the world's croplands are so badly managed that they are losing topsoil at the rate of about 7% per decade. In the rich world, it is likely that the alarms bells can be heard and the crisis averted. It is the poorest countries of the world, trapped as usual by poverty of opportunity, which may continue towards catastrophic decline of fertility.

Banishing wilderness

Whilst in one sense wilderness is increasing around the world, since desertification of arid and forest lands is leaping ahead (see **Cooking, Hamburgers** and **Peanuts**), the amount of wilderness which each of our new citizens will be able to enjoy is likely to be very small, if wilderness means land untouched by man.

Environment damage: African elephants range over land that is becoming desert.

What are presently virgin forests will probably – and with luck, sustainably – be pressed into service as we learn what productive activites are viable there. Many pastoralist herdsmen, living a wilderness life, are being pressed to become sedentary farmers, in a process which may one day bring vast areas of land into productivity (but may contribute, as now, to further desertification. See **Livestock** and **Peanuts**).

The next decades will see the exploitation of the least hospitable places on earth, especially at the South Pole, and it is an open question whether international laws will be forged in time to make the process orderly and equitable for the world's citizens. Meanwhile, if our young citizens would like to marvel at the animal denizens of our earth's wilderness regions, then in that department too they are likely to have far less diversity to enjoy (see **Condors**).

The partly good news

The numbers the world must support need not rise inexorably: people can and do choose to limit their procreativity. Moreover, the world has an immense capacity to grow food (see **Irrigation**). Indeed, there is no correlation between rising populations and falling per capita wealth: there are many countries with both steeply rising populations and rapidly increasing per capita wealth (Kenya, Tanzania and Pakistan amongst them). Increasingly, people of all political and economic persuasions are stressing the importance, above all, of sustainable agriculture for the world's billions. Reports from the United Nations, the World Bank, the International Monetary Fund, or a liberal charity such as Oxfam often show a wide consensus on the view that the planet is likely to be a successful place – more or less – if peasant agriculture finds a way forward.

Political and educational restraints stand between peasants and high productivity. Given the will, the world could support far more people. Scattered through this book are examples of the small signs and schemes which suggest that our future might be bright. Technical difficulties are legion, but they do not appear insurmountable. Political and cultural difficulties are likely to prove more obdurate.

Nonetheless, it is good news that much that needs doing to increase health, nutrition and shelter in the world is simple, at least technically. Much of the good to be done depends on getting messages through to ordinary, and often very poor people. The Third World need not fall prey to smoking-related cancers (though tobacco firms are promoting that imminent epidemic, see **Cigarettes**). Peasants appear to be far more productive than communards; land ownership by individuals is going to be more important than state-directed collectives.

Many small tractors do more for farming than a few big ones. People can build more and better shacks for themselves than governments can provide high standard apartments. A mere $5 will provide infant immunisation against many killer diseases. A $1 jab providing immunisation against rotavirus diarrhoea (a bit like scours in cattle) was reported in early 1985 as being on the cards, with a possible annual saving of 1 million babies. Breast milk is usually better for babies than anything to be found in expensive bottles or cans. Sugar, salt and water are a better cure for diarrhoea than pills. Good husbandry is a better pest killer than chemicals (see **Jeans**).

The well-being of the economies of most poor countries usually depends on finding ways of ensuring that money gets through to small-scale farmers so that they can husband their immediate resources for greatest productivity. But how can rich traders or political bureaucrats be persuaded to allow this to happen? And how can poor governments be persuaded that subsidising their urban employed, at the expense of starving their rural millions, is less productive in the long run than allowing their farms their proper health? How can the urban poor be persuaded of so hard a truth?

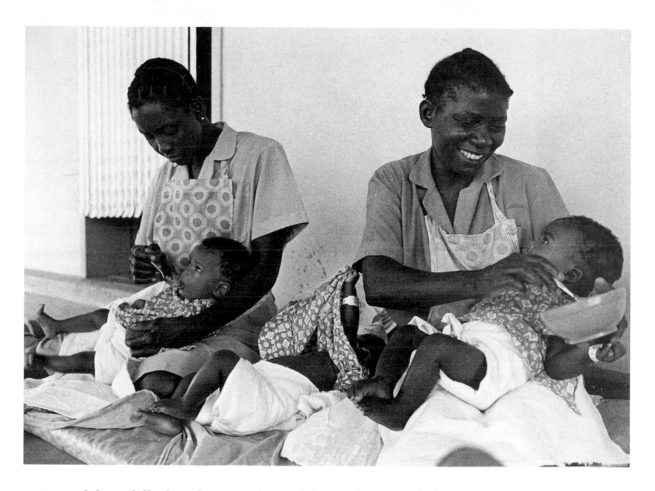

Beyond these difficulties: how can the rural farmers be persuaded to do the communal work which ensures survival for their grandchildren? Peasants around the world have shown themselves to be fairly resistant to co-operative or command schemes. This is a fundamental problem for reformers, and a severe dilemma. The communist world knows how to make people do communal things unproductively; the capitalist world in theory motivates producers, but has no mechanism to ensure that the productive also undertake socially responsible activity.

Do the politicians of the rich and poor worlds have the will to reform? Those in the wealthy world lack the generosity to want to help, and those in the poor prefer not to impede their own development prospects.

There is precious little point in pontificating, exhorting, or complaining about these subjects. Perhaps matters will deteriorate. None the less, there is no question of the immense wealth of the planet. There is clearly no technical difficulty with feeding and housing enormous numbers of people. Even the million new people born every 5 days could easily be accommodated given imagination and a certain amount of generosity on the part of those with power at every level in all societies around the world. Malthus – with his dire prediction that population will always outstrip food supply – does not have to be right, yet.

Nursing sisters feeding orphans in Central Africa: these babies' chance of survival is in marked contrast to that of children in rich countries.

19

2 Jobs: keeping the new world busy

"The growth of Japan's economy is likely to slow down . . . owing to a decrease in the growth rate of the labour force . . ."

Japanese population expert

Governments around the world have sought economic development, which they have usually expressed in terms of productivity per capita. This is a peculiarly bad way of solving the world's difficulty in feeding, sheltering and employing people. Of course, governments are not as powerful as is often assumed, especially when they are hand in glove with the upper classes in their country. As a result it is often the interests, or less pejoratively, the world view of the affluent which predominates in the councils.

Pursuing modern industrial development is in almost every case a very bad way of employing people. Poor countries usually find themselves growing crops (see **Peanuts** and **Coffee**) in order to buy foreign exchange which they invest in technologies designed in the rich world at a time when employing people seemed not to be a high priority (or something which would flow from economic growth as conventionally judged).

Thus, many poor countries pursue an industrial agriculture (throwing or pricing peasants off the land) and decrease their own national self-sufficiency in food in order to buy equipment which is itself designed to employ as few people as possible. It is hard to see this as anything other than the effect of self-enrichment by those who have power (who are generally the only people in poor societies to benefit from Western-style development), combined with the powerful myth that if poor nations do what rich nations have done, they will themselves become rich.

In one vast Brazilian beef ranch (see **Hamburgers**), which covers about twice the area of Luxembourg, the full-time employees were reported to number a mere 135, with another 400 employed at the peak season. By one count, small farms employ 5 times more people than large ones do. Small farms also tend to produce more per hectare (see **Peanut**), yet round the world they are under-capitalised compared to the 'new image' large farms.

Aid agencies have not always helped. They have, for instance, encouraged poor nations in the use of large tractors which are employed by the bigger farmers to impoverish the smaller men, whom they can then buy out. A flight to the city of unemployed land labourers in many parts of the world

Computer assembly workers in Oslo, Norway, 1980

has meant that **irrigation** works are collapsing for lack of labour, valuable soil conservation work such as terracing is neglected, and small **dams** which could provide energy and jobs are not built, whilst mega-schemes surge ahead.

Many of these small-scale projects are social. That is, it is in no single person's interests or capacity to perform them. It is a matter of public policy. Already there is anxiety that China's liberalisation of economic policy may be undermining the 'social' or command work which villagers undertake on common-value infrastrucure schemes such as **irrigation**, without encouraging the pooling of a share of profits for future works.

In the rich world, modern technology has both displaced workers and vastly increased the capital investment which will be required to create new jobs (see **Computers**). Interestingly, the contribution of the great technologies of the nineteenth and twentieth centuries in Britain make the point. The nineteenth-century railways contributed, as does modern North Sea oil now, about 4% of gross national product, but the railways employed over 2% of the population, whilst the modern oil industry manages only 0.1% directly, and perhaps 0.2% all told.

In many British industries, robots and computers have been introduced almost as a result of the recession. Some unions, fighting for the few jobs that remain, and keen on high wages for their declining membership, have accepted new techniques on the factory floor. One engineering firm has so modernised its plant that even with an economic upturn it would be able to expand production by a quarter without increasing its manpower.

In one Rolls Royce aerospace plant, one eighth of the previous workforce, allied with new technology, can build engine parts with a 20% saving in costs per unit, and repay its capital cost inside a couple of years, even in a depressed market. Though a booming economy would certainly create a demand for new workers, it would also encourage the investment which would enable much production to be automated to an extent which dis-employed people.

Clearly, those jobs which can be done by machine, will be. It was always so. One study reckoned that in 1850, 94% of the total energy used in US manufacturing industry was human or animal. By the mid-1970s, the population had tripled and the proportion of human and animal energy used had shrunk to 1%. It will require a self-conscious realisation that many jobs are not appropriate to machines – especially repair and craft work – to keep people in work. Creating real jobs in these industries will require deliberate purchasing choices by consumers. They demand a change of ethos from acquisition to making-do.

Finding a way forward

It will require as much courage and imagination on the part of poor countries as in rich ones to face the next century, which will be one in which sustainable agriculture and industries which employ large numbers of people will have to be developed. Neither are as profitable to elites as standard twentieth-century techniques but without both, a combination of inequity and starvation will lead to desperation in poor peoples.

The way forward: a people-minded agriculture

"In 1885, on a 420 hectare farm, 12-14% of the area was needed to feed the horse teams and full time manpower numbered 37, including 10 horsemen. The ratio of land to workers was 11 hectares per man, or less than a third of the 1970 figure of 37 hectares per man."

Gerald Leach
Energy and Food Production
(IPC Technical, London)

The rewards of a people-orientated agriculture and industry are there to be seen. In Zimbabwe, until independence, the white-owned farms had less than half the country's farmland, but produced more than three-quarters of the country's crops. Now, the far more numerous farmers in the usually inferior 'tribal' land have been encouraged by higher prices and increased government advice and investment to produce more than 4 times their previous output of some crops.

Even these spectacular gains will be hard pressed to feed the growing population, and the flight to the cities will tend to create in many countries dangerous unemployment.

In the Philippines, rice paddies employing many people in round-the-year cultivation have been proved very successful. In South Korea, reafforestation programmes have been successful (see **Cooking**). China's small-**dam** schemes have been famously successful. But all of these have depended on a degree of coercion which is unacceptable elsewhere. It is the business of attracting people to unglamorous craft and manual work which may prove the biggest stumbling block to high-employment strategies in rich and poor countries alike.

As oil prices rise, one of the great creators of unemployment, some of the advantages of machinery over muscle power will decline. Moreover, the rewards of recycling, reuse and repair of goods will increase: these employ people rather than energy. It has been reckoned that a well-made car, built to last 20 years or more and so amortise the energy inputs in its material requirement over a longer period than is the case with our throwaway cars, might employ nearly twice as much human labour as is currently the case.

However, in the rich world especially, the **computer** and the robot will help to create a society in which fewer people have jobs in original manufacturing. They will also take the edge off the employment prospects of the services sector, which the West has increasingly looked to as a source of growth. There is a vast need for appropriate technology, that is, in part, technology which makes manual work pleasant as opposed to technology which displaces it.

The black economy

In the poor world, the black economy predominates in many countries. It has been estimated that in the poor countries of Africa and Asia only 1 in 10 adults work regularly for wages, and in Zaire it was estimated that out of a population of 25 million, only 1.2 million had steady, paid work. For the rest, subsistence agriculture, payment in kind, or trading provided people with a living.

In many countries the informal economy is well established and does a good deal to allow even those who do not have formal work to retain self-respect and at least some income. Thus, a city like Cairo is an obvious hive of activity where few people seem to have nothing to do, even though official unemployment rates are high. In Western countries there is already a thriving 'black economy'. In Britain the black market is reckoned to be about 5% of the tax-paying, registered production and that figure may be as high as 10% in the US.

The domestic economy

Beyond the 'black' economy, there is likely to be a boom in the 'domestic' economy. In rich countries now facing recession and further long-term unemployment prospects, there is every probability that the dependence of families on financial earnings in order to provide goods and services for the household will shrink. By one estimate, about a quarter of household

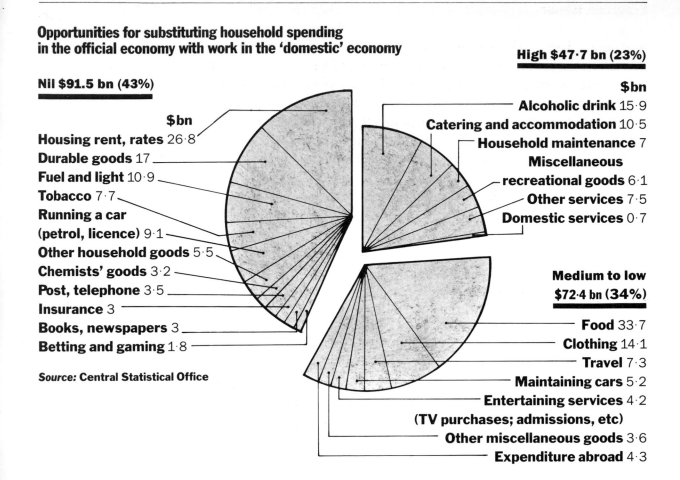

**Opportunities for substituting household spending
in the official economy with work in the 'domestic' economy**

High $47·7 bn (23%)

Nil $91.5 bn (43%)

$bn
Alcoholic drink 15·9
Catering and accommodation 10·5
Household maintenance 7
Miscellaneous
recreational goods 6·1
Other services 7·5
Domestic services 0·7

$bn
Housing rent, rates 26·8
Durable goods 17
Fuel and light 10·9
Tobacco 7·7
Running a car
(petrol, licence) 9·1
Other household goods 5·5
Chemists' goods 3·2
Post, telephone 3·5
Insurance 3
Books, newspapers 3
Betting and gaming 1·8

Source: **Central Statistical Office**

**Medium to low
$72·4 bn (34%)**

Food 33·7
Clothing 14·1
Travel 7·3
Maintaining cars 5·2
Entertaining services 4·2
(TV purchases; admissions, etc)
Other miscellaneous goods 3·6
Expenditure abroad 4·3

expenditure which currently goes into the formal economy is readily available for at least partial substitution by household production. Drink, restaurant food, household maintenance and recreation are all high on the list.

With rather more effort, a further 34% is available for substitution in varying degrees by personal production or performance. For example, home manufacture of clothing, cycling rather than using the car or train and camping rather than using hotels are all possible savings.

Healthy living (better diet and so on) and a development of informal education in the community and home rather than in institutions might make a major impact on the need to earn money. However, we have a long way to go: the workless in Britain at least are still hoping for a return to conventional life. One survey of 1,000 unemployed people found that two thirds of them had developed no new interests during their period of enforced leisure, and another found that the jobless devote less time to politics or voluntary work than the employed.

Exporting labour

In colonial days, rich countries employed the land and labour of poor countries by annexing them. Cash cropping round the world now does much of that work still, even in countries which are politically independent. But in a further development, the use of migrant labour, rich countries have been able to import labour from poor countries. They are able to pay them rather low wages, but for families waiting at home the remittances from a family member living abroad can seem a bonanza, or at least an enormous boon.

The great growth in labour-exportation came during the late 1970s and is now tailing off (and did so by the mid-1970s in the case of European labour-importers). In this way rich countries can export their recession and, by sending their poorest workers home, buffer themselves from its worst effects.

Taking all developing countries, the percentage of export earnings which came from labour-exportation doubled between 1970 and 1982, even though it had peaked by the latter date, and now stands at about 1.7%. It is running at about $22.6 billion for the entire developing world, but some countries earned more from their workers abroad than any other export, and in several the earnings sent home represented half the foreign exchange earnings. In Egypt, for instance, workers' remittances from abroad were double the country's merchandise exports in 1980, and the average worker abroad each year sent back about 4 times the per capita gross national product.

An Egyptian fella who can raise the necessary $100 for a passport earns between $1,000 and $1,500 in the Gulf in 6 months. This people-export has taken 3-4 million Egyptians abroad (mostly to Arab countries, with about an eighth to Europe). Egyptian peasants have seen their average income rise by 9% a year since 1976. Rather a large proportion of this wealth has gone into capitalising new agriculture on small farms (some of it with government aid sponsored by the US). Meanwhile, the raised expectations have meant that better-off landlords have been unable to employ local peasant labour at much less than $5 a day.

The Chinese have exported labour very successfully, and with complete indifference as to the politics of the employing nation. Of the 35,000 Chinese workers abroad, some are building railways in Iran and others **dams** in Iraq. Although the Chinese state takes 70% of the modern coolie's salary, the worker can earn $150 a month for himself, which is 5 or 6 times his earnings at home.

There has been a compulsory mass exodus of foreign workers from northern Europe, and even the Middle East oil exporting countries are sending their fellow Arabs home (in some cases to go further afield, like Pakistan, for yet cheaper labour). Between 1977 and 1982, 90,000 foreign workers took repatriation grants and left France; up to 200,000 foreign

A Singhalese village blacksmith
in Sri Lanka: traditional craft
employment.

workers were thought to leave Germany during 1982; Iran had rid itself of
150,000 foreign workers between the fall of the Shah and 1982; and Iraq sent
home 80,000 Pakistanis between 1980 and 1982.

Of course, the lot of the expatriate worker is often miserable. Separated
from his family, he will often live in a dormitory. France has 300 such foyers,
the condition of some of which has been described as terrible by the Mayor
of Paris' office.

The poor countries pay a high price for these worker remittances. In many
cases they are exporting their best brains, who would ideally be at home
spearheading the development of well-run agricultural or industrial
development. Often, the Third World countries are exporting hard-won
education. Thus, by importing brainpower, the rich countries save
themselves huge education bills, since a graduate costs in cash terms (but not
in relative values in the two parts of the world) about 3 times more in the rich
world than in the poor. Other studies suggest that some rich countries gain
10 times more from imported brainpower from poor countries than they
spend on educational assistance to those countries.

The value of a job

It may well be the issue of jobs that most divides the rich and poor societies of the world. In the rich world, we may be close to an age in which work will have a declining value in many people's lives. The **computer** and robot will banish many jobs and many people will 'commute' by computer into their offices. In the rich world one might posit that wealth distribution will have to be radically overhauled for two reasons: on moral grounds, because machine-made wealth has a habit of drifting into the pockets of rather small numbers of people; and practically, because huge numbers of unemployed people will not stand for seeing their position deteriorate indefinitely. The upshot may be a generous, easily available state income for people whether seeking work or not.

But the poor world has not reached the first stage of the industrial revolution, whose successive stages have put the rich world where it is. The Third World would be wise to avoid the route the rich world took – that of industrial job provision in factories – and look instead to that peasant agriculture the West undervalued until it was long gone. But with our insights and technology, poor countries can leapfrog the constant tendency first to find people jobs and then to work towards disemploying them.

The West is probably going to give up the idea of jobs in favour of people contracting to provide services, either within the market or voluntarily. The poor world may be able to develop in such a way that many more people own the factors of production: land, tools, seed, and so on.

In the rich and the poor world alike, the dominance of the idea of jobs may diminish in the face of wiser, freer ways of making a living.

The partly good news

The migration of Egyptian workers to Saudi Arabia (often illegal for the poorer amongst them, who use pilgrimages to Mecca as a means of skirting the law) has had several unexpected effects on village life at home, according to Fatma Khafagy (*Middle East Research and Information Project Reports*, New York and Washington, June 1984). She notes that in at least one village she studied, where nearly half the men were away, it was the women who pressed the men to take work abroad. Although the additional workload on the women was heavy, they relished the extra income (much of it wisely invested in productive equipment) and came, after a period of adjustment, to enjoy and appreciate (as did their husbands) their handling of new responsibilities.

Both men and women seemed to embrace the changing role of the women to become joint household heads, household managers and child rearers (the men had previously seen to the discipline of the children). Thus, it may be that labour migration becomes a powerful force for allowing women greater freedom and responsibility in Egypt.

> "In many cases, the wife encouraged her husband to take the risk and travel without a work contract, after the successful experiences of other emigrants made them regard emigration positively. The wives were also able to influence their husband's choice of purchases and investments."
>
> **Fatma Khafagy**

3 Bread: the staff of life; how it is grown and sold

THE average Briton consumes around 765g of bread a week. In the US the consumption is a little below a half of this, but in the US, around 20% of bread consumption takes the form of rolls and buns (as against about 5% in the UK), reflecting the hamburger and hot dog habit there.

Bread in the rich world is a product whose consumption has much declined. In the 1930s bread was far more important to diet in the UK than it is today, and poor people were spending 12% of their food budget on their 1.8kg weekly bread consumption. (The rich ate a relatively slight 1.4kg and spent only 3% of their food budget on doing so.)

The person who earns the family's living, or the major part of it, remains, however, the 'breadwinner'. 'Man shall not live by bread alone' remains a perennial text about our corporeal and a spiritual survival. Bread is a deeply symbolic, as well as a nourishing product.

Patterns of change

None the less, 100 or so years ago, for generations of relatively advantaged Westerners, and for some who were far from advantaged, brown bread – much commoner then, and becoming so again – was a symbol of poverty and deprivation. As soon as possible, the bread was 'improved' (actually, debased) by being whitened. The addition of powdered chalk saw, and still sees, to that.

In Britain, by the beginning of the eighteenth century the bread which had been eaten for generations (made of brown or whole wheat in the south and of barley, rye or oats elsewhere) was giving way to white bread, in a habit which saw the working classes follow a fashion which was *de rigeur* amongst the upper classes.

Further change was taking place. Just as poorer people had brewed their own beer but soon resorted to the public house, they now ate baker's bread instead of making it for themselves. (They more often brewed **tea** instead of beer, as well.)

The family's adults would be seen as wage-earners: first the husband was turned into a wage slave, with less and less recourse to his own land and animals; then the woman, too, was turned into an earner, and pressure of time often forced her to renounce baking. The era of the shop was inaugurated when the family ceased to bake and brew in their own house. By the 1840s, Engels was reporting that white bread and **tea** were the staples of the poor classes, as they had only a century before been sure signs of affluence. As the foremost historian of British diet, John Burnett (see **Reading List**), remarks, 'What had been mere adjuncts at the tables of the wealthy now constituted virtually the total diet of those who could afford no more.'

There were several causes beyond fashion for the move away from home baking. The notion of buying a uniform product, whose whiteness was equatable with refinement, was clearly attractive. Firewood (see **Cooking**), essential in good and cheap quantity for home brewing and baking, was scarce and expensive almost everywhere in industrialised Britain (as it now is round the world). It had been turned from a freely available forage material into a commercial crop; the enclosure of commons and woods had seen to that.

Brewing and baking took time, and the wage class had even less of it than the peasant class. They also required space, and the urbanised Britain which was emerging offered no spare space to the poor. Ignorance must also have played its part. It is a distinctly modern understanding that brown bread, with the wheat's bran intact, is a healthier food than highly milled flour. (One of those who first worried about the new roller milling of flour was Canon Hardwicke Rawnsley, who incidentally also saw that Britain would need a National Trust to preserve fine land and houses from destruction.)

By the turn of this century, UK researchers were recording that even working people were, for the first time, spending more on meat (see **Livestock**) than on cereals, and that this was the case even in the poorer counties (then, unlike now, in the south of the islands).

The changing image of bread

Cereal consumption in general has declined a great deal in the West. In the UK it is down from around 110kg a head per year at the turn of the century to about 55kg now. Bread consumption in Britain fell by a quarter in the 1960s and 1970s, though the consumption of brown bread is rising (up 17% in the past decade). Brown bread is losing its minority status. Even in the past few years the proportion of white to brown bread consumption in UK has shifted from 4:1 to nearer 3:1, a trend probably reflected also in the US, where, in the late 1970s, brown bread accounted for only a fifth of total bread consumption.

Independent small bakers in Britain have broken the trend away from local shops towards few, large supermarkets. Their brown and granary bread has helped to revive interest in old-fashioned loaves with firm crusts and fluffy insides.

White flour contains about 72% of the original wheat from which it is made. Whole-wheat flour, by definition, must contain the entire wheat weight, including the bran which is supposed to be a useful contributor to our diet by giving us roughage. In many countries white bread receives additives by law. In other words, the dietary damage which people would have sustained from their taste for over-processed food is mitigated at the state's insistence.

Energy and the loaf

"Give me, for a beautiful sight, a neat and smart woman, heating her oven and setting her bread! And, if the bustle does make the sign of labour glisten on her brow, where is the man that would not kiss that off, rather than lick the plaster from the cheek of a duchess?"

William Cobbett *The Cottage Economy* (London, 1832)

Of the energy needed to produce a loaf of bread and get it into the customer's hands in the shop, only 20% goes towards growing the wheat needed. Milling the wheat takes roughly 13%, the baker uses 64% and **packaging** the modern, wrapped loaf takes up almost 10% of the required energy. But should a person decide, as many might, that they want to go and pick up their loaf by car, there would be a further hefty energy-taker. In a British car, 2km would add 8 megajoules of heat requirement to some 20 megajoules required by a 1kg loaf.

Under UK agricultural systems it would require about 2.4m² to grow the amount of wheat required for a loaf, (a little less than 1kg); that area of land would receive about the same amount of energy that an entire hectare of Philippine rice paddy receives in a year. The hectare of paddy would produce around 1,500kg of rice, with a dietary energy potential about equal, kilogram for kilogram, with that of wheat. But British wheat fields, lush with energy inputs, produce almost 3 or 4 times the amount of protein per hectare that a low-input but warm-climate Third World agriculture provides.

A US wheat hectare produces well over twice the amount of protein that a wheat hectare in Uttar Pradesh does, and consumes roughly the same amount of energy. However, the Indian field, using bullocks and human sweat, employs hardly any fossil fuel amongst its 7 gigajoules per hectare (of which well over two thirds is delivered by the beasts) whilst in the US the vast majority of the energy input is from fossil-fuel derived sources. The Indian field system employs 100 times more human labour than the US does.

Wheat, aid and African farming

The world grows more grain (wheat, and coarse grains such as maize, barley, oats and so on) now than ever before. The 1984 bumper harvest in the prosperous grain countries (USA, Europe, Canada, Australia and, more marginally, Argentina) yielded 69 million tonnes of wheat from the USA

Growing wheat 19.4% — Tractors and machinery 5.8% · Fertilizers 11.1% · Drying, sprays 3.0%

Milling wheat 12.9% — Direct fuel and power 7.4% · Other 2.1% · Packaging and transport 3.3%

Bakers 64.3% — Direct fuel and power 30.2% · Other items 17.3% · Packaging 9.0% · Transportation 7.8% · Shops 3.4%

alone, and a further 238 million tonnes of coarse grain. There may have been something like 130 million tonnes of wheat stockpiled around the world at the end of 1984. In 1973, there were only some 70 million tonnes of any sort of grain in stockpiles.

The glut is in large measure the result of government policy: the USA subsidised its wheat farmers by $4 billion in 1983, and the EEC supported grain to the tune of $2.5 billion. The two subsidise their farmers very differently: the USA pays farmers not to produce, which helps to keep competitors in business by reducing supplies and tends towards keeping prices high; the EEC pays its farmers to produce grain, which increases supplies that are dumped cheaply around the world, and thus tends to decrease world prices.

As drought strikes Africa and adds its toll to the world's starving and malnourished, the first impulse of caring people in the rich world is to suggest that they should be the poor world's granary. This would be fundamentally bad policy, even if the rich world were generous enough to undertake it, but may be unavoidable in periods of crisis. It is an irony that it costs more to store grain than to distribute it to the starving.

The wheat surplus of the rich world costs governments a great deal of money, and is an expensive way of feeding Africans. Moreover, it is not stable as government policy may change at any time (it is changing fast in Europe), and prices are fluctuating wildly.

Africa needs to grow more of its own food, and in such a way that its people are employed (see **Jobs**) in economies which are relatively self-contained, though not entirely. Some cash crops can work efficiently for poor countries, and could with luck be made yet more useful (see **Coffee** and **Tea**). However, when it trades its commodities abroad, Africa tends to sell cheap and buy dear.

Energy required to produce 1 kg white loaf.

A breakdown of energy inputs to a 1 kg (2.2 lb) white, sliced and wrapped loaf shows some surprising hidden costs. Just under 20 per cent of energy consumed is in growing the wheat; all but three per cent of the rest is in processing, packaging and transport.

When some African countries trade abroad, the business of growing and trading their cash crops tends to be conducted by the affluent and the bureaucrats who have discovered means of creaming off the best part of the profit. The dilemma seems to be that while it is difficult to get African goods on to world markets in such a way that it would benefit the peasants, it is also difficult to get development aid to African peasants to help them grow for home consumption.

If rich countries want to be generous towards Africa, they need to find methods of funding peasant agriculture as it moves from primitive subsistence farming into a new, more productive but sustainable future. The alternative, as currently perceived, tends to suggest that we ought to be far more generous in direct food aid. In practice, the donor countries are not generous enough to do so on a long term basis at prices which Africa could afford. Moreover some of the recipient governments are not good at ensuring that the needy get the grain except in the direst emergency when their operations come under intense international scrutiny.

Direct food aid has the effect of disrupting the burgeoning markets for food in the receiving countries, which disrupts the peasant agricultural scene. But more than that, at whatever level of generosity the rich world can contemplate, our aid ought to find a balance between filling starving bellies *and* ensuring that there are fewer of them in the longer term.

Probably, the real tragedy of the situation is that the developing peasant agriculture of some African countries is fundamentally at odds with the interests of the elite sectors of the population. Thus it may simply be enormously difficult for the rich world to ensure that its aid is distributed in the most productive way, namely into the hands of the peasants to help them grow food. Meanwhile, direct food aid is spasmodic and disruptive, but crucial in periods of intense crisis.

Index of efficiency: what fuel goes in – what food comes out. Units of fossil energy input per unit of protein energy output for various foods.

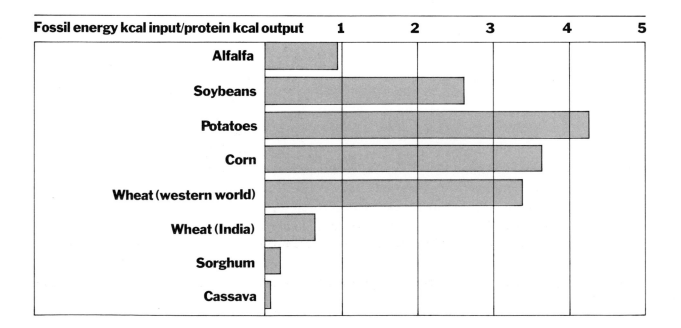

Fossil energy kcal input/protein kcal output

	1	2	3	4	5
Alfalfa					
Soybeans					
Potatoes					
Corn					
Wheat (western world)					
Wheat (India)					
Sorghum					
Cassava					

4 Tea: leaves, empire and poverty

For the British, tea is a very particular institution. It is a national drink, an Asian concoction which has uniquely embedded itself in the national consciousness. Behind the daily cups of 'char' (from the Mandarin and Cantonese Ch'a) there lies a trade for which the British have a particularly important responsibility which has survived from their early days of involvement, when the East India Company held a monopoly. Much of the tea (from the Amoy dialect, T'e) the world drinks today is purveyed by British firms and comes from plantations set up under British rule and rules.

About half of the world's 1.8 million tonnes of tea production is drunk in the countries of origin, whilst the rest goes into international trade. Asian countries produce around 75% of the world's tea, but British or part-British firms trade about 70% of it. Between them, 8 European and American firms dominate the growing or marketing of 90% of tea traded to Europe and the US.

Brooke Bond has a 45% share of the UK tea market. The company's chairman received a 1984 pay rise of nearly 30% – an increase of $35,000, itself around 60 times the total annual wages of one of the plantation workers who are indispensible to his lifestyle. The chairman now earns $154,000 a year, and lives in a company-owned house in a fashionable London district, which he rents for $700 a year.

Of the vast trade in tea which British companies undertake, only 200,000 tonnes is actually imported into this country, and of that 24,000 are re-exported. None the less, the British have a special affection for tea, with a per capita consumption of around 4.5 kg of tea a year, closely followed by countries with British traditions such as Australia, New Zealand and Canada. British consumption, per capita, is more than twice the turn-of-the-century level. One survey puts it at about 6 cups of tea per day, about the same as that in China where the whole tradition started. Tea constitutes about half an average Briton's liquid intake. India's large total consumption of tea (around half of its 600,000 tonne production) is made up of relatively small per capita consumptions.

Japan is a large producer and consumer of green (unfermented) tea, and increasingly grows and exports for the US, as does China with something like 6.2 million hectares of land down to tea (though much of the tea produced does not turn up on official statistics).

Although there has been a decline in the direct involvement of British firms in the growing of tea (there were 2,000 British tea plantation bosses in north-east India 30 years ago, whilst now there are only a handful), the insistence of the British and other Western markets on cheap tea at any price must shoulder a heavy share of the blame for the tea-pickers' plight in Asia and the newer plantations of East Africa.

Carving up the cuppa

The tea and hot water components in a cup of tea cost about 1¢ to the consumer who has caught on to the American habit of drinking the very cheapest tea in the form of tea bags.

Since we buy tea which has been dried and fermented where it was grown, a little over half the price of a cup of tea is returned to the tea-producing companies. Western and especially British trading firms add 25% to the price of tea in blending and packaging, whilst transport and retailing add a further 25%.

However, a very 'soft' market, brought about by the over-production attendant on there being poor nations competing for a share in a rich nation market, and plentiful labour, have made the tea-pickers' condition particularly poor (though some firms now point out that their pickers' wages have increased in line with inflation). Even in India itself, the cost of the leaves from which tea is made accounts for about an eighth of the price of a street-stall cuppa.

The (rising) supply of tea outstrips the (slightly falling) demand for it. The world price for tea has fallen by around 25% in real terms in the last decade. A tonne of tea would buy, in early 1983, less than half the amount of oil it would have bought in 1975.

The new producing countries, such as those in East Africa, are not keen to enter into production quotas which alone might help stabilise prices and encourage increased wages and reformed labour conditions. There *was* a price hike in some teas in 1983 because the Indian government saw a supply squeeze when its home consumption of tea rose and its home production could not keep pace. Such a hiatus is, however, regarded as routine and cyclical. India imposed export bans, sooner than face the political problems of high domestic prices. This raised the price of tea to Britons, who prefer the same sort of tea as India's people. The price increase enriched Brooke Bond substantially.

Plantations in Sri Lanka

In Sri Lanka (which with India supplies nearly half the British tea, and which is dependent on tea for more than half its export earnings) the tea industry has wrought much human misery and a good many economic distortions. Sri Lanka exports almost all its production.

Tamil tea pickers in Sri Lanka.

When the British introduced tea plantations to Ceylon (as it then was) in the late nineteenth century, they had difficulty finding Sinhalese labour to work the plantations. Their solution was to import Tamil workers from India, of whom there remained at least 0.5 million in 1980, in spite of several years of repatriation by the Sri Lankan authorities who have largely taken over the tea estates.

The position of the Tamils in Sri Lanka has always been precarious. Most of them are stateless and voteless and often the victims of racialist attacks. In recent years an old Clyde-built steamer, the *Ramanujam*, has been shipping Tamils across the 43 km-wide strait between Sri Lanka and India, 400 at a time (355,000 between 1964 and 1981). These people have been 'processed' back into Indian society (actually, to unemployment and homelessness, though with a loan of $200) through the same Mandapam camp in which their forefathers spent a quarantine period before being shipped to Sri Lanka. The plantation Tamils, being mostly poorly educated and powerless, are the scapegoat for Sinhalese bad feeling against Tamils in general; it is the higher

35

caste Tamils of north Sri Lanka amongst whom there are dreams of separatism. None the less the tea pickers suffered dramatically when rioting disrupted tea production in 1983.

And so it is that life for most Tamil tea pickers is one of barracks ('line houses') in which families live in 1 or 2 rooms, and may have the luxury of a scrap of land and a cow. There may or may not be a tap on each line of 24 rooms and often the girls of the family are deputed for the trek to the nearest well. Firewood for **cooking** comes from aged tea plants. The entire family may work in different jobs around the plantation. Picking takes place between 7.00 am and noon, and from 1.30 pm to 4.30 pm. Women are crucial to the plantation's work, and their children are often catered for in creches and schools.

Pay in 1982 was around 46¢ a day for women, with men getting more, on a piecework basis, and working children rather less. Half of the children at work on Sri Lankan tea estates are under 14 (the legal minimum age). Child labour may well be an issue about which the rich world takes (when it thinks about it at all) a rather precious attitude. However, these youngsters get little out of the early commitment to a productive life: 85% of under-age plantation workers are suffering from malnutrition, whilst mortality rates are twice those for the island as a whole.

. . . and Bangladesh

In Bangladesh, the tea-picking women, whose wages are around 23¢ a day or less, have been described by the Roman Catholic Justice and Peace Commission as 'slave labour'. In Kenya, a tea picker may earn 69¢ a day, but that is on a Brooke Bond estate, who are amongst the best payers. Brooke Bond have reported falling infant mortality statistics (about half the national average for the countries in which they operate) in recent years on their estates.

The people who run tea estates have always claimed that they must do well for their shareholders and that they must do, in Rome, what the Romans do. Even if it were true that it would be in some way peculiar to pay tea pickers the kind of rate which is proper to the purveyors of luxury goods to luxury markets and which could easily be afforded, there is clearly no reason at all why rich consumers should not pay more for a commodity and make sure that those who work to produce the commodity are decently employed and housed.

. . . and Kenya

Kenya is high on the world list of inequitability. The poorest third of its people earn around 6% of total income while the top 2% take nearly a third of it. Since independence, the country has tried to encourage smallholder production of tea, which has more than doubled its hectarage since 1971.

The large plantation estates, owned either by foreigners or an African elite, have about 20,000 of the 75,000 hectares down to tea. But they produce half the output of the commodity, with yields that are a half or two thirds higher per hectare than their smaller competitors. Moreover, the corporations which are involved in tea trading and growing often in effect force the smallholder to grow the difficult, labour intensive, better quality teas on his average one third of a hectare, but they do not have to pay a premium for this hived-off intensive work.

By an astonishing irony in a country where peasants are being forced off the land and into mass unemployment in the cities, there is a severe shortage of labour in some tea-growing areas. This shortage is often caused by delays in payments to farmers, who consequently cannot pay for help picking their crops. Moreover, payments to farmers for their tea have been halved in real terms in the last decade and Kenya's ability to buy imported machines in exchange for tea has slipped by an average 5% a year.

Tea troubles

The tea industries of the East have recently been suffering from bad underinvestment. Input prices have been rising fast, but not received prices. Plantations – especially those no longer under foreign ownership – have been putting off necessary investment in the pruning and replacement of plants. This work, although bad for immediate cash flow, is, however, vital to long-term survival.

Packaging

Tea is a largely anonymous, homogenous product, in the sense that few consumers know or care where the tea they drink was grown. The vast majority of it is sold to be blended and packaged by famous firms who promote their products as best they may (for instance by the clever but demeaning use of chimpanzees in the famous Brooke Bond television advertisements which were begun in 1956). The rise of the British chain grocer in the middle of the nineteenth century depended crucially on the brand packaging of tea by people such as John Horniman and Thomas Lipton.

The packaging of tea allowed the public to develop a brand loyalty which spread to the entire shop where it was sold, and which overcame the public's distrust of 'loose' and unlabelled teas (and other products) which were then very commonly subject to adulteration by poisonous but cheap substances. The packaging of tea was thus seen to be very useful for the consumer.

But how much good has it done the producer? Branded teas place great emphasis on the value of buying a familiar national name, and trusting to it for the blending of teas which come from wherever they may be bought cheapest by the purveyor. The brand name effectively stands between the consumer and the producer and helps to make it difficult for the consumer to identify or empathise with the tea producer. Furthermore, tea bags, in which form we drink half our tea, encourage cheap, low-profit tea growing. Actually, we ought to be insisting on buying tea about whose provenance we know a great deal, rather than sheltering behind familiar brand names.

It should be possible for consumers to choose to buy tea which has been packed in the country of origin, and thus to allow producers in the countries concerned to keep a higher percentage of the high-profit value-adding blending, packaging and branding processes. Meanwhile, only 10% of tea from Sri Lanka is exported in packaged form.

It is often possible for rich-country consumers to buy tea from 'alternative traders' (see **Coffee** and **Address List**).

5 Coffee: taking the best land from peasants

THE 3 or 4 million tonnes of coffee which poor countries (and about 20 million people in them) supply to rich ones do neither party to the arrangement as much good as their high value to the former and high cost to the latter might suggest. Three quarters of the world's coffee crop goes into international trade, making it the world's largest commodity market, second only to oil.

Coffee is the ultimate cash crop. It was a crop 'invented' by Europeans (via its Middle Eastern origins) for growth in far-flung nations. Only introduced to Brazil in the 1870s, coffee quickly became the country's leading export. In 1978, Brazil produced about 20% of the world's coffee, and until recently the crop earned three quarters of that country's foreign exchange. Columbia had a tenth of the production.

Enough coffee for a year's supply is currently in storage, as a result of international agreements which try to stabilise prices. However, all too often the agreements break down or are evaded. Artificially high world prices have invited producers to overproduce and cheat the system, whilst artificially low prices have encouraged consumption, which again offers strong temptation to evade regulation. Many African countries producing coffee are discriminated against by the international coffee cartel in which producer and consumer nations arrange prices and quotas. Although they are members, their voting power is slim.

Amongst consumers, which largely means importers in this trade, the United States has led the field for decades. The US imports about a third of the world's crop (something over 1 million tonnes), closely followed by West Germany, with almost 0.5 million tonnes.

In Britain, the average consumption of coffee is more than twice what it was even in the 1950s and the increase is largely accounted for by the development of instant coffee. Moreover, as eating out became more a habit than a luxury, and sophistication spread within the population, 60% of respondents (instead of the 40% in 1947) recently told researchers that their ideal meal ended with a cup of coffee.

Instant coffee, which now accounts for around 90% of coffee consumed, is hugely expensive in energy. Roasting, grinding and processing it takes around 18,000 k/cal per kg, which makes it 10 times more energy extravagant than a **fish** finger and 100 times more so than ice. The coffee in your cup of instant coffee cost about 60% of the price charged by the retailer (some of this 60% is accounted for by transport), whilst fully 10% of the price goes towards promotion.

It does us no good

Caffeine, one of the few active ingredients in coffee, has always been a component of almost any 'tonic' drink. Actually, it is no such thing. It is a brain stimulant, which works particularly powerfully on the 'wakefulness' system (as the sixth-century Arabian priest who is said to have discovered the bean's effect noted: it kept his goat awake at night).

Caffeine affects digestion, exacerbates stomach problems, and has been implicated in problems of circulation. Though it is still added to Coca-Cola (see **Carbonated Drinks**) pregnant women have been warned against it by the US Food and Drugs Administration. Moreover, Australian researchers believe they have found another component in coffee (not caffeine and not found in other beverages such as tea) which is addictive and which has an opiate effect on the brain, but which eludes direct identification at present.

Coffee and its producers

A slump in Europe or America has often led to the collapse of the world market price of coffee. There is a notorious fluctuation in supply of the produce as farmers try to cash in during times of strong prices. For instance, demand for coffee in Britain between 1801 and 1841 rose from 0.3 million kg a year, to over 10.5 million kg. Desperate to keep up with the bonanza, coffee plantations, especially in Brazil, flourished.

Soon after the turn of the century, there were 20 million sacks of Brazilian coffee on the market annually, and only 12 million sacks'worth of demand for them. Across the following decade, 40 million sacks of coffee were burned. And the phenomenon continued, never more so than during the slump of the 1930s. In recent years, partly due to the present recession and partly to increased worldwide production, coffee prices have been low. Prices for coffee fell by 40% in just 2 years, between 1980 and 1982, when there was an annual surplus of 12% of coffee production. (Some coffee, such as Jamaica's Blue Mountain, fetches 4 times the average world price.) The year 1984 saw higher, but very unstable, prices which were set to fall. A poor harvest in drought-stricken West Africa contributed to shortages of supply. The USA, especially in election year, pressed hard for low coffee prices.

"Rivers of the coffee areas are highly acidic and contain 7,000 milligrams per litre (mg/l) of organic pollution. This extraordinarily high figure can be compared to 500 mg/l for other types of industry."

Earthscan, of Colombian rivers near coffee-washing plants, *Water, Sanitation, Health — for All?*, 1981

Raw coffee beans being washed, Uganda.

There's a lot of money growing in Brazil

São Paulo, with a population of well over 12 million, is one of the poorest and fastest growing cities in the world. Ranged around it, especially to the north west, is the world's most concentrated coffee-growing activity. Following its introduction in the nineteenth century, coffee became a powerful force for the wrecking of the luxuriant but fragile virgin forest in the area of what was then barely a city. The land was used, without fertiliser or fallow period, until exhausted, and the plantations moved on.

Over the years, a gang-labour system of cultivation has developed. Under this system, labourers live on a landlord's estate for a period of time, and are allowed to grow some susbsistence crops on their own account (which depresses their wages). However soil exhaustion tends to break up estates and lead to the formation of others.

Coffee plants need a 4 or 5 year period before they come into production, and are subject to Brazil's variable climate. There are therefore great fluctuations in supply of the crop. A drought in 1940 reduced the crop to a quarter of the previous year's. Following frosts in 1976, many hectares of land went out of production altogether and are now under **sugar** and soya. A frost in May 1981 halved Brazil's output of coffee. Moreover, most coffee strains, especially the prized Arabica, are highly susceptible to pests and diseases, notably the coffee rust disease which wiped out the Sinhalese crop in 1869. In Brazil, severe frosts in 1984 threatened the harvest in 1985.

Coffee growers in Brazil must pay half their earnings to the government's monopoly trading organisation although recently growers have been allowed to keep more of their earnings. The organisation has been offering consumer countries cut-price coffee, in order to increase the country's market share.

Bean politics

With a third of Nicaragua's export earnings coming from the coffee crop, 100,000 people are needed for harvesting. But many students, who would normally have been beginning the work in November 1984, were called to the capital Managua to defend it against a possible invasion. At the same time, opposition guerrillas (supported by the US) were threatening to take action against the crop if they were attacked by the army.

Coffee in Kenya

Coffee plantations were expanded in Africa in the first decade of this century in an attempt to break Brazil's strong market position. One fifth of Kenya's land is in the highlands, which are ideal for coffee. The land is so fertile that a family of 6 can live on the produce of half a hectare. Overall, Kenya has 25 hectares of fertile land per family. Often, however, even a relatively fortunate mother of several children will be left at home trying to earn a living from a quarter of a hectare, whilst her husband seeks work in a city such as Nairobi.

Colonial British authorities insisted that no Africans could own large tracts of Kenya's best land, and allowed only squatter labour there. Today, well over half of the best land in Kenya is given over to cash crops, employing labour at the rate of about 69¢ a day. Cash crop firms, many of them African-owned, find it easy to buy the best land, especially from smallholders who get into hopeless debt trying to find cash for schooling (only primary education is nominally free) or medical care.

Of Kenya's rapidly growing population, 85% live in the country as agriculturalists. Increasingly however, many are forced into those marginally productive areas, where few high value cash crops are grown, and where 1 or

Watering coffee seedlings, South India.

2 hectares of land produce less than the quarter hectare of good land a family might have had before selling up. They cannot be careful farmers as they are too poor to take care to rest the land between crops, or to leave trees standing as good soil protectors (see **Cooking**).

Ecology and cash crops

Worldwide, the picture is no better. Over-exploitation of the fragile tropical soils of the Caribbean for coffee amongst other crops (see **Sugar**, **Bananas** and **Cigarettes**) and a similar pattern of land ownership have forced subsistence farmers off their land, to a slash-and-burn agriculture in the highland woodlands.

One authority on Brazil's agriculture has stressed the absurdity of the state coffee authority bullying farmers, who would know better, left to themselves, into monoculture (in which a farm grows coffee, coffee and coffee, rather than a stable variety of crops). Such farming leaves crops open to disease and soils dangerously prone to erosion. Ironically, it took genetic material from an African forest to provide Brazilian coffee growers with a strain which could better survive variable weather and leaf rust.

Small can work

Peasant farming does not have to be entirely subsistence; conversely, cash cropping does not have to be run by landowning elites. In Cameroon in West Africa, an enlightened goverment (which had benefited from better than usual relations with its ex-colonial master, France) has pursued a policy of aiding small farmers, though this has been done at the cost of higher food prices in the cities. The small farmers must, however, pay increased taxes when world prices are healthy.

Half of the country's coffee production now comes from small farmers and their contribution is rising. In Rwanda and Burundi, holdings with up to 100 trees, alongside other farm produce, are very common. Their inputs are low, as are their outputs.

Smallholders, working through co-operatives, produce 60% of Kenya's coffee. Their yields per hectare are about half those for large plantations (though with enormous regional variations), but their produce is of a far higher quality. It is the inefficiency of the co-operative and state organisations which buy from the farmers that above all inhibits the expansion of earnings for small farmers. Payments are delayed because of cumbersome accountancy, and inflation during long waits for payment often accounts for a 20% fall in the real price received by the smallholder.

According to the International Food Policy Research Institute in Kenya,

> Transaction costs for a smallholder are high. To deliver small quantities of cherry (ripe coffee berries) often means long waits in queues, sometimes far into the night. The farmer has little recourse if he is told to regrade. Obtaining payment sometimes involves several more days of waiting in line. These additional fixed costs for the smallholder arise because he is only allowed to sell to the co-operative society where he is registered, which consequently enjoys all the privilege of a monopolist.
>
> Farmers are not able to reconcile deliveries and payments because of the spreading out of payments. The system is further complicated by credit and advances.

A wide range of deductions are made from farmers at source, which further diminishes the real price he receives for his crop. But none of these are written down in a form which the farmer can check, and he has no effective channels of complaint. The upshot is that whilst a plantation receives around 90% of the export value of its coffee, the smallholder's take hovers at around 60%, and that with tremendous uncertainty and delays. If these could be overcome, the result could be higher effective prices for peasants, and smallholder yields could be raised by 50% in a very few years.

There are great difficulties to face, however, in increasing coffee production. One is that the long-term prospects for coffee prices are not good, though there may be market opportunities for specific coffee types. In any case, the foreign exchange which countries earn from cash crops is used to buy imports, and the price ratio between their produce and their purchases has been in long and steep decline.

Curiously, perhaps, the position in capitalist or left-wing countries is often very similar. They are both plagued by bureaucracy, for instance. The state buying and exporting agencies in capitalist Kenya swelled their bureaucracies from 114,000 to 230,000 people in the decade up to 1981, but probably with increases in inefficiency in doing so rather than the reverse. Whilst university education may be a flawed indicator of efficiency, it is notable that, in 1980, in the essential co-operative movement of around 20,000 employees, only 200 had degrees, and only a quarter of managers had attended even a fortnight's training in the co-operative college.

Meanwhile, in left-wing Tanzania, the government's avowed purpose of increasing large scale co-operative ventures has always met strong peasant resistance. The peasants have not been able to see the advantages in communal work schemes, especially as the payouts have not always been equitable.

The vast and occasionally draconian government insistence on 'villagisation' attempted to force a co-operative vision on peasants who would more likely have raised output in response to price rises than to visionary reorganisation.

Poor coffee (and other) prices over the 5-year period up to 1982, combined with rising oil prices, meant that Kenya's agricultural export terms of trade fell by over 27%. More starkly put, it now takes 4 times more coffee to pay for a barrel of oil than was required in 1975.

Any poor country has to balance the potential of foreign exchange earnings from cash crops against the need to grow food for its own population. About a third of any foreign exchange earnings Kenya might make from agricultural cash cropping goes to buy inputs (fertiliser, expertise, etc) from abroad, but that is a far smaller proportion than would be the case with industrial development.

Yet urban populations (swollen by poor agricultural earnings) like and need cheap food, and militate strongly against high prices for subsistence produce. Meanwhile, the huge majority of Kenyans who are agriculturalists need high prices for their produce, and need to get their hands on a far higher proportion of its worth.

Moreover, in Tanzania, the 80% of the country's population which is agricultural receives only 12% of the country's development investment, and only 2% of that total goes to peasants.

Meanwhile, Tanzania's bureaucracy performed even more badly than Kenya's. In the decade up to 1980, the Tanzanian peasant's share of the price received for agricultural crops slipped from 66.5% to 49%. Much of the rest was increasingly soaked up by the apparatus which was supposed to be marketing produce to the producers' advantage.

Across the years 1973 to 1980, the coffee producers of Tanzania (who contribute about a third of the nation's export crop value) saw the real price of their product decline by 18.5%. Bureaucracy doubled in Tanzania in the first half of the 1970s, and now consumes 16% of the national budget.

A picture of dependency.
A country may produce only a small percentage of the world's total production of a crop, but be very dependent on it. See Costa Rica, for example.

Country	Population (m)	Output (1000mt)	% of crop-land under coffee	% of world production
Brazil	128	1003	2.5	20
Columbia	26	840	19.2	17
Indonesia	153	266	2.6	5.4
Costa Rica	2.3	113	17	2.3
Kenya	18	95	5	2
Tanzania	19	55	2	1.1
Jamaica	2.2	1	1	.02
USA	232	1	.0005	.02

Things you can do

There is no need to buy coffee only from the large firms whose policy of indifference towards the land and workers is reinforced by consumers' compliance. It is possible to buy coffee which has not been produced in the standard way. Much of the coffee (about half) produced in Tanzania is grown on the slopes of the Kilimanjaro region (with EEC aid), under a system in which smallholders are encouraged to keep cash cropping in their own hands.

Though there are very few such plants in Africa, there is an instant processing plant in Northwest Tanzania, at Bukoba, and though its links with Traidcraft (see **Address List**) people can buy 'Campaign Coffee' which is produced and processed in an industry which does far more than most to profit local people without distorting land values and national agriculture.

6 Sugar: the sweet and sour cash crop

SUGAR is refined from a sticky substance found in the stems, and particularly in the lower part of the stems, of a tall grass. In its refined form it is a dangerous commodity which could very easily be replaced in dietary terms. However, some of the 110 million tonnes of sugar produced annually is used in the production of alcohol and, should health anxieties harm its marketability as a food, the crop may have a future in providing energy for cars rather than for people.

Sugar is mostly grown as a luxury part of the human diet. Few people, apart perhaps from mountaineers, need their energy in a form which is so implicated in health problems. Indeed, it has been suggested that high, quick doses of sugar contribute to obesity in a peculiar way: they fool the digestive system into believing that it is still hungry, and create an artificial hunger. However, in most rich countries, and many poor ones, people have acquired a strong taste for it. In the Sudan (see **Jeans**), for example, a 60% price hike in 1982 precipitated urban rioting.

In the Western world, sugar consumption now runs at over 50 kg (some put it at about 60 kg) per capita annually. This amounts to around 6 heaped tablespoons per day. In rich countries the consumption is falling, but the picture amongst the better-off of the world's poorer countries is very different. In Egypt, where sugar is used in the vast quantities of tea people drink, average consumption is close to 30 kg per capita and is still rising. India exports only 1 million of its 6.4 million tonne production. World consumption has risen by about 1 million tonnes a year this century, amounting to around 3 times the quantity produced at the turn of the century.

Food manufacturers in Britain and many other countries use a large amount of sugar in their products. Since there is often no indication on the label as to the exact quantities of the ingredients, sugar is often involuntarily consumed by the purchasers. Even in countries such as the US, where product labelling is more explicit, the consumption of sugar is made difficult to renounce by its ubiquity in almost all convenience foods.

In Britain, the consumption of sugar per capita was in the region of 11 kg per year in 1850, and 36 kg by the end of the century. It was estimated to be about 57 kg per capita per annum by 1960. Since then, direct domestic purchases have been dropping because of health fears, but the total consumption figure declines very much more slowly because of involuntary consumption.

Although artificial sweeteners have gone some way towards denting the sugar consumption of rich countries, there exists another substance which is reckoned to be a far healthier means of satisfying the sweet tooth. Corn sugar, which is high in fructose, holds one tenth of the US sweetener market.

"The crystals which so beguile us are pure sucrose, a compound ($C_{12}H_{22}O_{11}$) which can be extracted from any vegetable matter, including grass."

New Statesman,
19 September 1980

The sugar growers

Sugar is not merely a useless crop, it is a crop with a unique record of human misery. Conceived by colonialists for cash cropping, it was historically dependent, first on slave labour, and later on indentured, often Indian labour, especially in Mauritius, Fiji, Guyana and Trinidad. Between 1670 and 1820 sugar was Britain's biggest import.

Countries such as Cuba (third in the league table of the world's sugar-cane producers after India — mostly a home consumer — and Brazil), Mauritius in the Third World, and France in the rich world, are very dependent on sugar exports. Cuba sells nearly 5.5 million tonnes of its 7 million tonnes of exported sugar to communist block countries at well over 10 times the world price.

Cutting sugar cane, Guadaloupe.

The French only took to sugar production, in the form of sugar beet, after Napoleon realised that his country would be denied access to Britain's colonial crop. Sugar beet is not economically competitive with cane sugar, but is only grown, following Napoleon's lead, as an import-substitution crop. The EEC was a net importer of 1 million tonnes of sugar a decade ago. Now, as a result of subsidising its uneconomic sugar beet producers, it exports 5.4 million tonnes at knockdown prices, which helps depress Third World sugar markets.

The EEC now has reason to regret the hundreds of millions of dollars spent subsidising inefficient production of the crop by French, German and British farmers. Several rich countries have signed arrangements with the poorer world which go a little way towards stabilising prices at levels which would probably obtain naturally if it were not for the EEC's policy of subsidising surpluses.

The declining terms of trade

> "Two hundred years after enslaving people to work on sugar plantations, rich countries are enslaving them again by ruining those same plantations and the poor countries that rely on them."
>
> **The Economist, August 10, 1985**

With 100 producers in the market, world overproduction has led to dangerously depressed markets in recent years, despite conventions (often flouted) which attempt to impose quotas. After a brief spell of good prices in the mid-1970s, the price of sugar fell by over 70% between 1980 and 1982 and is expected to remain at very low levels. By late 1984, sugar had slumped to about one tenth of its 1980 price. The early 1985 price of 8¢ per kg was less than one third of the world's most efficient producer's costs. There is now a vast stockpile of sugar, equivalent to half a year's consumption. The declining terms of trade are reflected by the decline in the buying power of a tonne of sugar. In 1975 a tonne of sugar could have been exchanged for 41.8 barrels of oil, but in 1983, it would have bought a mere 4.1 barrels.

The terms of trade have been working against the Third World sugar producers for several years, and any decline in the market will worsen their position. Only quotas can improve the inequities of the market. America pays 3 times the market price to favoured suppliers, and Mauritius, which depends for two thirds of its export revenue on sugar, gets EEC linked prices for its huge exports to EEC countries. Indeed, only about 20% of the world's traded sugar is sold at the world price. The rest is traded in a complex, fragile and unstable series of deals, often between rich countries and their favoured-client Third World countries. However, many of these long-term contracts are coming to an end and the shock waves of low world prices are likely to hurt many more poor countries soon.

As the price crumbles, the international arrangements which are intended to firm up prices by imposing quotas are widely ignored. As so often (it applies to **gold** through Russia's wheat purchases), the world commodity markets are strongly influenced by the enormous buying power of the USSR in world markets for foods that it is not always able to grow. In late 1984, the

Crushing sugar cane with bullock-driven press, India.

Soviets were reckoned to be about to go on to world markets for sugar. That seemed about the only bright spot in the commodity's immediate future, as it faced a drastic price collapse yet again.

Moreover, many countries do not benefit from favoured-producer deals. Australia produces 3.6 million tonnes of sugar a year, and exports almost 3 million tonnes of it. Yet, despite being extremely efficient, Queensland state alone expected to see 10% of its farmers driven to the wall in 1985.

Within overall declining terms of trade, many producing peasants in 1984 were earning a declining share of the price their governments received for their crop (see **Births** and **Coffee**). Many small growers in the Philippines have been suffering badly from those classic symptoms caused by greedy governments, low domestic crop prices and overvalued local currency. Some 60,000 have recently lost their livelihood, whilst others are paying 50% interest on overdue loans. The 0.5 million workers in this industry have always been desperately poor and times have never been worse.

The partly good news

Fiji, since its independence, has succeeded in building a sugar industry which, comparatively, mitigates many of the hazards of cash-cropping. According to a 1982 study by Frank Ellis of the University of East Anglia, the maintenance of small farms has done a good deal to ensure that growers can weather weak markets: they invest less in high-volume machinery and are therefore caught out less in depressions.

Under an arrangement negotiated by the British judge Lord Denning in the early 1970s, a fixed and comparatively generous proportion of the price gained for sugar gets into the growers' hands, whence it is mostly spent inside Fiji. Thus they avoid 'import leakage', under which foreign earnings effectively return to the rich world through imports by the cash-cropping country.

7 Carbonated Drinks: marketing fizz

A SYRUP made from a medley of ingredients, including a West African nut, the potentially narcotic leaves of a South American jungle bush and large quantities of sweetener (see **Sugar** and **Glass of Water**) must seem an odd recipe to symbolise the American dream and gain international success. None the less, two companies, Coca-Cola (the coca is that leaf, and cola the nut) and Pepsi-Cola have performed the feat, aided by enormous advertising campaigns. Successful it has been. Soft-drink consumption, and with it consumption of sweeteners, rose almost 3 times between the early 1960s and the late 1970s, from 51 litres to 128 litres per person per year. In the same period, US consumption of **coffee** fell by 30% whilst H_2O (see **Glass of Water**) consumption per person fell by a quarter.

This extraordinary consumption of exotic pop in the US adds up to 400 cans per person per year, much of it consumed by the 13-24 age group. (It has been estimated that each of the crew of US Navy ships accounts for around 5 cans per day, many of which are simply thrown over the side.)

Finding markets with fizz

However, the post-war demographic surge of youthful mouths is now over, and a lower and lower percentage of the profits of Coca-Cola come from the sales of soft drink in the US. This factor, combined with a low 10 can per capita annual consumption and very youthful population in the Third World, accounts for the interest shown by soft-drink companies in expanding sales abroad.

The success of soft drinks abroad has been due, in part, to the ingenuity of the franchising operation which provides a means of selling a standardised product whose quality is easily controlled. A syrup is made by the owner and shipped to the bottlers, wherever they are. Almost all the ingredients are useless or dangerous (though the coca in Coca-Cola is now a detoxified resin without narcotic effect). In the poor world, they are richly inappropriate. There are no oranges in Coca-Cola's Fanta Orange, but the drink is often sold to countries such as Brazil, which ranks amongst the world's largest orange producers, though its population is commonly and chronically afflicted with Vitamin C deficiency.

There is another very unattractive side to franchising. It allows the company that produces the sugary liquor to employ as bottlers local people who have sometimes been unscrupulous. They have sometimes understood their local economy so well that they have exploited labour drastically.

Fizz or food

Some countries have gone so far as to recommend bans on some soft drinks since they were being fed to babies instead of **milk** by mothers who had been duped by their unsophisticated reading of advertisements.

Poor people the world over (see **Cigarette**) have been successfully hooked on the image of being consumers. Where public and healthy water supplies are rare, the antiseptic, macho, rich-world-approved, bottled soft drink is an accessible alternative and parody. Of course, the poor man in a poor world can reach for a Coke, squandering his money whilst he does so; what is ironically sure is that he could not – by his solitary effort and small expenditure – achieve clean water supplies for his family. That requires corporate effort.

Marketing fizz – South Africa.

Fiji is dependent upon sugar for about 80% of its foreign earnings. The crop contributes approximately 16% of the country's gross domestic product and employs about 20% of Fijians (around 40% of agricultural employment) in highly seasonal labour. The crop occupies one third of Fiji's agricultural land and accounts for about half its agricultural output. But less than 20% of the country's production of half a million tonnes of sugar comes from larger farms (over 10 hectares).

However, though cane cutting as an occupation has seen quite large percentage increases in pay in the past decade (as money accruing to growers has increased), in recent years it has been heavily eroded by inflation. Cane cutters earn about $4 per tonne of cut sugar cane. A day's work usually yields an average of about 1 tonne per man, earning a seasonal (and therefore often an annual) income of about $700, which is taxed at between 2% and 3%. But this earnings figure has less to do with a man's potential productivity than with the gang and quota system under which sugar cutting is organised. An average grower's farm might yield him a profit of around $2,000 once he has paid about $9 per tonne to the labourers who produce and cut his crop (though, especially in depressed times, he will often 'employ' his own family for these tasks).

So far, Fiji has wisely resisted the mechanisation of its sugar-cane farming. Mechanisation seldom makes production cheaper for growers, though it can make the process 'conveniently' free of employed labour. However, the fluctuations of the sugar market impress themselves mostly on the landless labourers, who are the first to be shaken out of employment, and many of whom are badly in debt to their employers. Fiji has suffered in the price collapse of sugar: in spite of favourable deals, in 1984 real incomes from sugar were half their 1977 levels.

Energy into sugar versus energy from sugar

Something near 4,000 million litres of ethanol (alcohol) was fermented, mostly from sugar cane, in Brazil in 1983. That country aimed to treble this output by 1985. Because by-products of the cane can be used to fuel the actual process, there is a net energy gain of a factor of between 3 and 4. However, in the US, where at best sugar cane is at the outer limit of its climatic range, the energy return is negligible by any known process of alcohol distillation.

By the same token, though the production of sugar beet in the UK is fairly energy efficient (about 4 units of available energy for every 1 of input), the refining process makes a nonsense of this if the beet is to be turned into refined sugar: almost twice as much energy goes into the production of sugar from sugar beet as will be consumed by the end user.

For sugar cane itself, the energy efficiencies achieved depend dramatically on how much mechanisation is used. High-fertiliser production without the use of much mechanised power gives an energy return of upwards of 5 times the energy input. Add mechanisation, and energy efficiencies fall by half.

Drinking-chocolate powder	**73.8**
Sugar-coated breakfast cereals	**45.6**
Chocolate biscuits	**up to 38.2**
Packet muesli	**26**
Tomato ketchup	**22.9**
High fibre breakfast cereal	**12**
Carbonated drinks	**10.5**
Fruit yogurt	**10**

Percentage of sugar in selected foods

Diet and pop-poverty in the US

For many people in the West, fast food (see **Hamburgers**) provides up to a quarter of their diet. Fizzy drinks play their part in this phenomenon, although they provide energy and nothing else of diet value.

The following table compares the nutrients contained in 230 cc of cola drink as opposed to the same amount of orange juice. (**Coffee,** by contrast, contains very few calories but can be a useful source of niacin and iron to heavy consumers.)

	230cc Cola	230cc Orange Juice
Energy	401.03	468.37 kJ
Protein	0	1.75 g
Vitamin A	0	498.00 IU
Vitamin C	0	112.05 mg
Thiamin	0	.22 mg
Niacin	0	.75 mg
Calcium	0	22.41 mg
Iron	0	.25 mg

Orange juice can be a major source of vitamin C as less than half a pint gives about 1.5 times the US government recommended daily intake for an adult.

A **hamburger** with a fizzy drink will provide about a quarter of an individual's engergy needs for the day. The same burger consumed with a **Milk**shake is a good deal richer in other nutrients and provides almost half the riboflavin and calcium. By contrast to a hamburger-based meal, a single pizza portion can fulfil half of an indivual's protein needs, well over a quarter of needed energy, riboflavin, niacin and calcium, and score highly in the other nutrients as well.

8 Bananas: the upstart fruit

'STRAIGHT off the banana boat,' is an old British expression for an innocent, which refers to the wave of West Indians who immigated to the UK during the 1950s. Ships from the Caribbean carried descendants of the slaves British sea captains had bought or stolen from Africa – and bananas.

Bananas are the most prolific tropical fruit; perhaps 36 million tonnes are produced every year, of which about 7 million go into world trade. The typical banana has travelled 6,500 km between plantation and consumer. Some economies are dangerously dominated by the banana trade. Honduras, for instance, depends for 70% of its export earnings on its 0.7 million tonnes of exported bananas. Brazil is a far bigger producer of the fruit, but is far less dependent upon it.

Bananas were introduced to the New World, probably along with the slave trade, but did not become a large-scale commercial crop until refrigerated ships made possible the long transatlantic crossing, utilised as a ripening period. Bananas must be eaten within 3 weeks of picking. Although the fruit became a useful supplement to sugar plantations, rather few genetic strains were introduced, and the crop has always been susceptible to disease.

Worse, the banana plant is very prone to damage from high winds, and this makes its introduction to a hurricane region, the Caribbean, peculiarly ironic. The Jamaicans are now trying to recreate a banana industry. In 1980 their crops were devastated by hurricanes, in the wake of which their export of the fruit declined by more than a half. The banana plant's susceptibility to wind damage has led many producers to transfer their interests from the Caribbean islands to mainland Central America, thus spreading the blight of dependence upon the fruit to Costa Rica and Honduras.

There remain several countries with a very fragile dependence on the fruit, which has taken the place of sugar for many of them. Once a country is hooked on cash crops, change becomes extremely difficult. The Windward Islands, for instance, were persuaded in the 1950s by a Dutch family, the Geests, to begin banana plantations.

The family firm's fortunes, which are extensive and not by any means solely based on fruit imports, are still bound up with Grenada, St Lucia, St Vincent and Dominica. These countries signed exclusive contracts with the company, and their crops are carried to UK markets by Geest ships built with heavy British government subsidies. Dominica now earns more than half its foreign earnings from this one crop (which was devastated by hurricanes in 1979 and 1980). In competition with Fyffes, Geest's Windward Islands crop makes up 40% of the British banana market.

The cash-crop routine ensures at least a promise of regular income for the small farmers who predominate in the Third World, and certainly in the Caribbean. But part of the difficulty is that many of the products are now in great oversupply, and poor regions of the world are competing to outdo one another with their cheap labour, loose pollution controls and the orderliness of their social control.

Moreover, inflation has hit the rich world to the point where, though in 1970 the income received from selling 11 tonnes of bananas would buy a tractor, it would now take well over twice that amount of fruit. And though many things are cheap in the Third World, and in the Caribbean the climate is hot all year round, there is endemic malnutrition, since high-protein foods are not grown locally to any significant extent and are expensive to import – certainly compared with prices in the UK or US. Typically, mains water (see **Glass of Water**) and modern sewage disposal are rare, and intestinal problems common, especially in children.

However, any attempts by producers to mitigate their dependency on the banana market by forming 'unions' or guilds are stymied by the market place. Though Columbia, Costa Rica, Guatemala, Honduras, Nicaragua and Panama formed the Union of Exporting Countries (UPEB) in what might have become a good imitation of OPEC, and although the Dominican Republic and Venezuela joined up later, they could only speak for half the world's banana exports. Producers responsible for the remainder of the world's exports, amongst them Ecuador – the world's largest producer – would not join.

UPEB has tried to set up a marketing organisation, COMUNBANA, to handle its exports, but it has made small progress. In spite of its efforts and those of UPEB, the would-be monopolists still only speak for a tiny proportion of UPEB's bananas which are mostly sold through 3 American companies that effectively control the growing and marketing of 60% of UPEB members' banana production.

The growing nations normally receive something like 12% of the price that consumers pay for bananas. The most that might be said for the rich corporations which earn their living from much of the rest of the price of bananas is that they trade in a commodity whose success depends on its being cheap. There is no certainty that an expensive banana – one which gives a good living to producers as well as to traders – would sell in the market place.

In the 1967 the Filipinos decided to start growing bananas for export, especially to Japan, which had just eased its tariff regulations. In a couple of years, they took their export production from under 0.5 million to 23 million, and thereafter production rose by annual 500% and more, until the mid-1970s, when it contributed over 88% of Japan's banana imports.

As often happens with traded cash crops, banana plantations were soon ousting peasants – in this case, often tribal peoples – from good, and often public, reservation land and banishing them to steep hillsides. There was a good deal of armed land-snatching. Often, irrigation water was effectively controlled by the new plantations which had invested some money in improvement and took the investment as a claim to manipulate water supplies solely to their own convenience (though occasionally the peasants struck back forcibly).

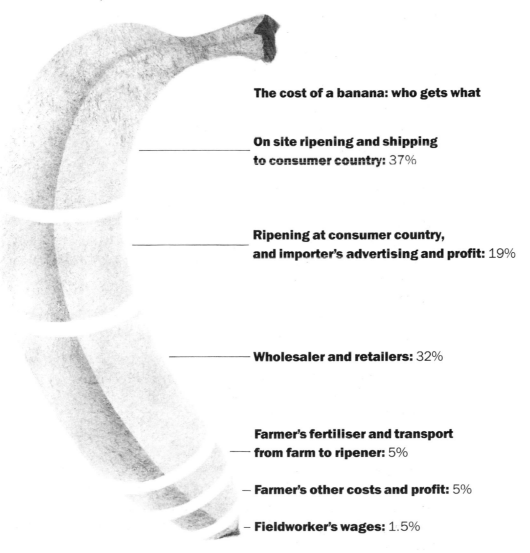

The cost of a banana: who gets what

On site ripening and shipping to consumer country: 37%

Ripening at consumer country, and importer's advertising and profit: 19%

Wholesaler and retailers: 32%

Farmer's fertiliser and transport from farm to ripener: 5%

Farmer's other costs and profit: 5%

Fieldworker's wages: 1.5%

In some cases, companies in the Philippines, partly in order to breach minimum wage regulations, have indulged in the *kabit* system. Under this scheme, an official and registered worker has a 'shadow', who does the same amount of work, with whom he must share his wages. In other cases, an entire family works for the price of the husband. Often, small growers are heavily in debt to the large companies which nominally trade for, but actually very effectively control, them.

Whilst the Japanese market became 'soft' through saturation, input costs (irrigation, pesticides, and so on) rose dramatically. At times, the Japanese actually paid for banana-plant destruction to stem the supply. Simultaneously, banana-growing land was, in the late 1970s, showing signs of nutrient deficiency, leading to reduced crops.

Getting off the treadmill

Meanwhile, even attempts to diversify out of banana production are controversial. Costa Rica's banana plantations are giving way to rows of African palm, used for its oil and resistant to disease and forceful winds. It is hoped that this oil production may eventually reduce Costa Rica's dependence on **coffee** (whose price fluctuated from $8 a kg in 1978 to less than $3 a kg in 1982) and **cattle**. But there are difficulties. Palm plantations are very profitable for their owners, usually American companies, but require half the labour of banana farms. Moreover, the oil crop is mostly used at home, which saves importing foreign oil but does nothing to earn foreign exchange. But the palm often revitalises fields which had previously been stricken by the vicissitudes of the banana trade, and its environmental impact is usually much less than that of banana plants.

9 Peanuts: oil, sandwiches and deserts

In America, peanuts mean sandwiches, sometimes, in the hands of imaginative kids, with jelly. In Britain, where, as in most parts of the world, their main use is as cooking oil, they summon up – in older heads at least – embarrassed amusement. In 1946 the British government, anxious about the shortage of vegetable oils after the Second World War, set up what was to be a vast scheme (1 million hectares was hoped for) of peanut production in East Africa

Tanzania (then Tanganyika) was to be home to a massive peanut-growing operation: but $42.5 million later, there were only a derisory 25,000 hectares under crops. Weeds, soil erosion, waterlogging (see **Irrigation**), disease and other problems all conspired to remind the developers that agriculture is a subtle business in which progress will usually be slow (there had been too little research and surveying behind the scheme).

The peanut, grown extensively in poor countries for export as cooking and salad oil, is a remarkably prolific crop: one hectare produces 240 kg of peanut vegetable fat per hectare of land. The same area of land produces 138 kg of soyabean fat, while the average cow produces only 42 kg of butterfat per hectare of food (see **Milk**).

Peanuts originated in Latin America and spread to Africa, India, Mexico, the Philippines and Asia in the hands of the Spanish in the sixteenth century. The stock from which a huge American production is descended probably came from Africa in the seventeenth century. Peanuts have been a successful crop for the rich US, where they make a useful source of protein for human and animal consumption. They are grown in careful rotation, usually with cotton. For many poor countries, however, they exemplify aspects of the cash-cropping trade, and also the difficulties in exploiting tropical soils.

Peanuts depend on sandy soil, in which they bury their seeds (or 'nuts', though they are actually beans); hence their other name, groundnut. They are often, therefore, grown on soils which are subject to wind and water erosion. Australia, for example, is suffering massive soil erosion in its subtropical areas which have been forced into overproduction, often of peanuts, by over-optimistic farmers.

The peanut trap

It is in the poorest hot countries of the world where the overproduction hurts people and land most. In the Sudan, Burkina Faso, the Gambia, Niger and especially in the world's fifth largest producer, Senegal, peanuts have recently proved to be a difficult crop on which to base an export trade. Senegal has 1 million hectares of peanut fields, from which it derives a third of its export earnings. Almost 100 years of production and increasing pressure to produce a crop, however poor, rather than allow a fallow period, has seen yields halved recently.

Falling world prices have created adverse terms of trade for these poor countries. Between 1960 and 1970, for instance, the terms of trade declined

A picture of dependency.
A country may produce only a small percentage of the world's total production of a certain crop, but be very dependent on it. Gambia, for instance, has fully a third of its cropland down to peanuts, but produces only 0.69% of the world's crop.

Country	Population (m)	Output (1000 tonnes)	Percentage of crop land used for peanuts	Peanut production as percentage of world total
China	**982**	**3873**	**2.47**	**20.84**
India	**686**	**5700**	**4.44**	**30.64**
USA	**230**	**1561**	**0.27**	**8.4**
Sudan	**18.9**	**800**	**7.9**	**4.3**
Cameroun	**8.6**	**120**	**5.0**	**0.64**
Zimbabwe	**7.6**	**115**	**8.9**	**0.61**
Mali	**7.0**	**170**	**9.7**	**0.91**
Burkina Faso	**7.0**	**78**	**6.4**	**0.4**
Malawi	**6.1**	**180**	**10.0**	**0.96**
Senegal	**5.8**	**700**	**19.1**	**3.76**
Guinea	**5.6**	**85**	**8.2**	**0.45**
Niger	**5.5**	**88**	**5.3**	**0.47**
Chad	**4.6**	**118**	**5.6**	**0.63**
Central Africa Republic	**2.5**	**128**	**5.9**	**0.68**
Gambia	**0.6**	**130**	**36.7**	**0.69**

by over 30%, continuing a downward trend which began in the 1920s. In some countries exports of peanuts amount to over 20% of their foreign earnings.

In Mali, more land is given over to peanuts and cotton (see **Jeans**) than is used for production of food for home consumption. But Mali's export earnings from cash crops do not cover the cost of importing food.

Worldwide, cash crops take up almost 0.75 million km². It must be assumed that many countries would be better off with an agriculture which fed people directly, or at least maintained a better balance between earning foreign exchange with their land and filling bellies directly from it. But that would require the landlord and governing classes in those countries to become uniquely concerned with feeding populations, rather than pursuing their own interests and only developing the kind of farming which potentially maintains their position. In Niger, the land under peanut cultivation has more than halved recently, as farmers switch to production for subsistence rather than cash.

Overproduction of many crops (see **Livestock**) has severely reduced the fertility of many arid and semi-arid countries. Grain yields in Niger, Mali, Burkina Faso and Ethiopia have mostly fallen, and sometimes quite dramatically. In central Sudan, for instance, 5 times more land is required today than was required a generation ago to obtain a given crop of peanuts. There was once a lengthy cycle of cropping and fallow periods during which the land could recover. The scrapping of fallow times combined with overgrazing have led the farmers into a doubly pernicious dependence on cash crops.

The Sahel study: a story with few villains

It is often difficult to get beyond patchy anecdotal evidence about the effects of different crops in a region. Luckily, in the case of the peanut, the work of Richard Franke and Barbara Chasin of Montclair State College, New Jersey, has fleshed out for us a historical perspective on how the patterns of agriculture have changed. In a classic paper, first published in *African Environment* (August 1980) and reprinted in *The Ecologist* (July/August 1981), they worked through a wide spectrum of interconnected factors which led up to the disastrous inability of the Sahelian countries of the sub-Sahara to survive a severe drought which began in 1968 and continued through to 1974 (see **Livestock**) and devastated many parts of Africa in recent years. The Sahelian countries were, they remarked, heavily dependent upon a very few exports. Niger, for instance, earned well over 60% of its revenue from peanuts and the country's markets were very concentrated, 83% of Niger's peanut trade being with the US and European countries. The authors disposed swiftly of one favourite way out of the problem of poor countries supplying rich ones, by suggesting that if the West had paid more for their peanut oil, they would, amongst other things, have encouraged even more damaging overproduction.

In some countries, peanut production had been traditional. In Niger, however, it had hardly ever been thought worthwhile, until the French colonial authorities and business interests decided to promote the crop. Unfortunately, peanut production was taken up in the areas around villages which were previously kept fallow against emergencies. Moreover, the introduction of peanut farming disrupted an ancient pattern of transhumance (stock movement) in which the nomads of the north of the country came south for a yearly spell, during which their cattle had a change of diet and gave their dung to the soil. Moreover, peanuts, as they came to predominate, were found to produce far less fodder as a by-product than many traditional crops.

The French authorities and commercial interests promoted peanut cultivation with loans and presents all through the 1950s. In the early 1960s, the peanut become one of the most spectacular examples of the green revolution, in which seed breeding brought about strains with huge productivity increases (during the middle 1960s, peanut production more than doubled with hardly any increase in land given over to the crop).

The French colonial authorities on the ground were often very worried by the phenomenon they saw around them, but were powerless to stop the growing dependence. Three years after one regional commander had been warned by the governor of Niger that no further land should be planted with peanuts because it threatened subsistence cropping, 50% of the region's farmers were none the less found to be between 50% and 80% dependent on peanuts for their income, whilst almost all the others were also heavily committed.

It was already becoming clear to agriculturalists that peanuts were a demanding crop requiring either large amounts of fertiliser or a fallow period of 6 years following 3 years of peanut growing in order to maintain fertility. The peasant cash-cropper was not receiving the sums of money which allowed him to arrange for such measures. The improved seeds, which had been bred as fertiliser-hungry, were seldom receiving the required dosages and were therefore degrading the soils yet more. As a result, the peasants were slipping deeper into debt to fertiliser and implement companies.

Meantime, by the end of the 1960s, France was easing back on its financial support for African peanut growers, undoing the machinery of subsidy which had wooed them into the crop in the first place, but not funding an escape route for farmers caught on the cash treadmill.

During the 1960s, the land which was taken for peanut production began to include grazing areas and the pastoralist nomads were being threatened on their own territory. Supported by the government, not least because their activities could be taxed, the agricultural peasants were encouraged onto land which the nomadic herdsmen needed for part of their seasonal transhumance. In several places, herdsmen were having to keep their cattle all year round on fragile, near-desert land which they would normally have used only in the rainy season. Moreover, the production of **livestock** was being encouraged, which meant that there was a growing number of animals living off the poor land. Come one of the periodic severe droughts, and there was no reserve of fertility in the land to support a quantity of animals and plants which was barely sustainable even in ordinary years.

Sorting peanuts, India.

10 Livestock: feeding animals instead of people

Man began as a hunter-gatherer whose relations with animals was that of predator or prey, and perhaps admirer or even worshipper, rather than – as today – that of manager.

Man annually farms around 150 million tonnes of carcass meat (including poultry) with an average annual per capita meat consumption in the world of something like 32 kg. In India, however, this figure is something like 2 kg and in China the figure is 10 times that, at around 20kg. In New Zealand consumption is about 10 times that again, at well over 200 kg. In the rich world, especially the US, different meats are fashionable at different times. Lamb and veal have seen dramatic declines, whilst beef continues its inexorable rise.

By weight of production there is as much pig as cattle meat (beef and veal), but the far more numerous pigs are very much easier to keep in vast numbers or individually in close confinement than are cattle. Similarly, although there are probably 6 or 7 times the numbers of poultry kept as there are cattle, cattle meat outweighs poultry meat by almost 2:1.

It has been estimated that there may be 1,300,000 million kg dry weight of terrestial animal biomass alive in the world today. About 4% of that is human weight (see **Birth**). But our non-flying domestic livestock (see **Milk**) represents a further 15% of the total dry weight, or about 200,000 million kg.

Thus to feed, haul or entertain ourselves we have arranged that for each of us there is almost 4 times our weight in cattle, pigs, sheep, and a small number of mules, horses, asses and sundry dogs and cats, in total about 3,000 million animals.

Cattle...worldwide diversity

Ironies abound. In India there are more cattle than in any other country. Of the world's total of 1,200 million cattle, 15% are in India, which produces a negligible amount of beef (their cattle are sacred and used as draught animals or for hide). In some countries, such as Costa Rica (see **Hamburger**) beef consumption per capita has fallen as the country's production has rocketed.

Man's first cattle seem to have been rangy, leggy, lean creatures which could get a living on poor ground. It is probable that the animals were mostly regarded as useful for haulage, and that they constituted a kind of emergency larder for the winter months or against crop failure. Also, they had the merit of utilising land which was too poor for tillage.

In many countries, cattle are seen as useful for exploiting marginal land. Hardy beef animals in Scotland, for instance, often come to maturity very slowly, but they utilise poor ground. On much marginal British land, suckler herds, in which beef animals are allowed pretty well an ordinary family life where the mothers rear their young, could make a profitable way of farming.

However, where grain is abundant, this principle is increasingly often overthrown and the cattle are subjected to various mixes of the range-bred/intensive-fed arrangement. Thus, in the western states of America, where the prairies were largely colonised by Europeans with herds of cattle, there is still a tradition of herds ranging widely over poor or medium quality grasslands. But they are increasingly becoming the nurseries for a vast feedlot industry, with its alarming profligacy of resource use.

Crops for cattle: grazing or feedlot?

A surprisingly large proportion of the world's grain production goes to feed animals. The figure varies, roughly according to the wealth of the nation concerned. The USA produces about 1,300 kg of grain per person per year (leaving aside exports). Of this, only about 14% is eaten by humans while the rest is fed to animals.

A farming nation can only get a little over 2 kg of animal protein per hectare from its land when used for freeranging beef animals. If the land could be converted to feedlot beef (where most of the land grows grain for confined animals) and match the average American feedlot-system efficiences, it would achieve over 50 kg per hectare, or 23 times more.

There would of course be a price. The intensive feedlot farming system uses 178 times more fossil energy per hectare of crop-growing land than the freerange system. But even though a freerange animal 'wastes' perhaps a quarter more of its food in living instead of producing protein compared with a captive beast, the freerange animal is 7 times more efficient in its conversion of fossil energy into protein energy. This reflects the peculiar business of modern agriculture in which we have replaced the sun/soil/shit method of farming with a practice which converts fossil fuels into food, but does so inefficiently.

The 16% or more of US energy which is used in its food-production industries represents the equivalent of about 4 l of oil per person per day. This is well over twice the total per capita fossil-fuel take for the average citizen in the developing world. The US food industry's requirement for energy has doubled since the 1950s.

"In the US more than half the privately-owned rangelands are, because of overgrazing and related erosion, producing forage at half their potential or less. In many regions, especially in the Third World, pastures are declining to desert-like barrenness."

Erik P. Eckholm
Down to Earth (Pluto Press, London, 1982)

Cereals

	Total crop 1000mt	yield kg/ha	area down to cereals 1000ha
Australia	13577	835	16262
UK	21818	5412	4031
Netherlands	1380	6749	204
France	48074	4959	9694
Japan	14011	5308	2640
India	134145	1304	102857
China	306229	3303	92714
USA	339350	4409	76966
Burkina Faso	1282	588	2180
Botswana	22	139	160

Freerange or feedlot? The table shows the cereal production of various countries – a wasteful way to feed cattle. Below, cattle in a semi-arid area of South West Africa.

Often, two extravagances are involved: the first is to use vegetable protein to feed animals instead of people, and the second is to grow grain to feed the animals on land ill-suited to the crop. Of all the high and moderate quality farmland in the UK, only 8% is used to feed man directly.

Land in the wet south-western counties of Britain, or along river valleys which flood from time to time, has often been brought into grain production whereas it would, ecologically, be better suited to direct grazing of animals. Subsidised grain prices, however, make this operation profitable. Even so, the UK imports around 14 million tonnes of feedstuffs for its animals.

However, it can often be beneficial to grow crops to take to cattle, rather than allow them to graze freely. In the mountains of north-west India there have been a few successes in bringing steep, overgrazed, severely eroded hillsides back to life. The change is towards irrigated fields growing fodder crops and vastly increased yields of other crops for people, so that the hills can recover their vegetation. The difficult trick is to ensure that access to these schemes and their benefits is evenly distributed, so that ordinary peasants will make use of them.

Cattle and land

Man has domesticated cattle for something like 5,000 years. They seemed, often were, and still are an ideal means of utilising poor and often fragile land. On African, American and Indian deserts and hills, arid and semi-arid land has always been used for cattle ranging, especially in the absence of high-capital **irrigation** schemes. Cattle ranging for **milk** and beef is a major use of the one third of the world's land surface, in which more than 600 million people live, which is arid or semi-arid. Of these lands, 30 million km^2 are under direct threat of desertification. This represents over 20% of the earth's land surface, and is crucial to the sustenance of the 80 million people who live there.

Cattle and desert – especially in the Sahel...

The nomadic people of the Sahelian countries – Mauritania, Mali, Niger, Chad, Burkina Faso, and Senegal, for instance – maintained until recently a traditional system in which the numbers of animals were sustainable, even across fragile grazing lands, because of their constant movement.

Though Africa's 300 million inhabitants are matched by about the same number of cattle, they produce far less meat than the numbers imply. African cattle weigh, on average, less than half their rich-country counterparts. But there are fundamental difficulties in using high productivity, European-type cattle in Africa. Such animals do not usually graze very efficiently on African grasses, and, worse, they are very susceptible to drought and African diseases.

Part of the problem is that not merely does Africa have to feed more and more people, but there are larger numbers of animals to be kept on land which cannot support them. In the years 1968-73, one of the periodic droughts hit the Sahel; there have been 4 this century. The disruption of traditional, low-level grazing and consequent huge animal numbers, the cutting down of woodland for firewood (see **Cooking**) and the badly engineered **irrigation** schemes which had led to waterlogged fields all conspired toward disaster for the entire region.The sub-Saharan countries lost up to a quarter of a million people to starvation, and up to 4 million animals. Now, with drought seemingly endemic (it was repeated very severely in 1984 and 1985), the animal numbers are pretty much where they were before the catastrophe because of improved cattle health. They are well above sustainable numbers, and are very susceptible to drought. The pressure to increase animal numbers partly follows the increase in human population. The current annual growth in the Sahel is something like 1.5 million souls per year added to a 1982 population of around 60 million.

In some sub-Sahelian countries, the nomads, in competition with cash crops (see **Peanuts**) have had to relinquish their traditional movement of cattle amongst pastures (transhumance). They have become sedentary farmers, based around new waterholes, and often competing with outsiders for the newly drilled water.

Perhaps the best that can be hoped for in much of the Sahel is that the savannah grass and woodlands, and the less widespread forest, might be encouraged to re-establish themselves. It may be that the carrying capacity of the land will always be lower than previously expected, but it may conceivably be higher than it is at present, when the desert environment is increasing in response to attempted increase in production.

However, such a policy would require that the least politically powerful of all the groups in competition with one another, the nomads, be given priority and that they restrict their own numbers and the numbers of their cattle. No one has the smallest idea whether this could ever be achieved. There are some hopes of introducing a Texan-style division between the stock-producers in the north (who could be nomads with breeding herds) and the feedlot fatteners in the south, nicely near the profitable markets. Meanwhile the tragic equation of increased numbers of people and animals on a decreasing stock of good soil continues. Land that once carried at least some grasses, trees and shrubs turns to desert.

...and Australia

In the 200 years that Australia has been in the hands of colonial farmers rather than Aboriginals, one half of its topsoil has gone, and a third of the nation is covered by soil which needs concerted ecological restoration if its fertility is to be rediscovered.

Almost 2 million km² of arid land, and well over 0.75 million km² of less dry land have been overgrazed, by sheep as well as cattle, to the point of serious fertility loss. In the arid land of the continent, where there is virtually only animal-ranging and a tiny human population, 50% of the land has been severely damaged.

In the Gascoyne basin of north-western Western Australia, even well over a decade ago, 60 years of heavy sheep grazing was seen to have put some areas – about 15% – at risk of permanent degradation. In other areas, many farmers were finding that it was not profitable to continue to farm lands where the carrying capacity had suffered so severely. Some Australian rangelands, and millions of hectares of croplands, are affected by salinisation (see **Irrigation**), which has resulted from the elimination of natural vegetation.

11 Hamburgers: fast food myths and realities

IT is the proud boast of one American hamburger company, McDonalds, that half the adults in the US eat one of their hamburgers at least once a month. The enormous success of the hamburger is just one part of the Western world's infatuation with meat. Along with **fish** and chips, and chicken and chips, the notion of chopped-beef patties in a bun seemed ideally suited to consumers who wanted homogeneous, unadventurous, luxurious food, and to producers who wanted a food which required no skill and little expense to prepare and serve. The result was a product which contributed mightily to the average American's consumption of 120 kg of meat a year. Nearly half the meat consumed by Americans today is bought at fast food outlets. The American diet, dominated by the 300 kg of animal produce the average adult eats each year (see **Eggs** and **Milk**), is chronically wasteful of resources and good health.

It also produces, with 70 g of meat protein and 30 g of vegetable protein every day, at least twice the protein requirement of the ordinarily active individual. Half of this unnecessary protein contributes to fatty tissue and heart attacks.

The typical US hamburger meal (Big Mac or Burger King Whopper, french fries and one chocolate shake) delivers about 1,200 calories and upwards of 40 g of protein. The calories in an American quick snack are the equivalent of about half the total daily calorie intake of the average person in a developing country. However, there are many developing countries (Central African Republic, Zaire, Haiti and Sri Lanka amongst them) whose average citizen receives less protein from his total daily diet than the American does from his hamburger snack.

Oddly, though, nutritionists in the US are concerned that those youngsters who are receiving upwards of a third of their food in restaurants, especially fast food joints, may be in danger, because their diet is high in calories but low in vitamins and nutrients.

Even the Japanese, with their low protein/low fat diet, are succumbing. Their per capita meat consumption has quadrupled, from 17.6 g per day in 1960 to 70 g per day now. Beginning with the American military occupation after the Second World War, the Japanese have now fallen prey, as has most of the non-communist world, to America's friendly consumer 'imperialism', spearheaded there, as elsewhere, by the hamburger and McDonalds.

In 1960, the Japanese had a 40 in 100,000 death rate from heart disease; perhaps a Western diet will put them in the West German (225 in 100,000) or US (300 in 10,000) leagues. Meat production has almost trebled since the mid-1960s, and they are reducing their dependence on their previously dominant staple, rice.

There are two fundamentally different approaches to the modern production of meat for the Western market. One is to take the cheapest land available and graze it, often to extinction; the other is to pen the animals in feedlots and feed them food grown elsewhere.

Hamburgers or habitat?

The hamburger is heavily implicated in the destruction of the forests of the world. Running out of cheap enough land at home and faced with a massive meat demand, Western meat-buying firms turned abroad. From the woodlands of Africa to the rain forests of Central America, the toll has been a recurring pattern of devastated forest, ruined soil, starving local peasants and an enriched small elite in Third World countries (see **Livestock**).

Wherever cheap land is available, there is a modern pressure to graze animals, whose meat will seldom be cheap enough to feed the local peasants' bellies. There are limits to this exploitation. McDonalds and some other firms claim not to use imported meat in any country where they operate, though in the US, meat is not marked as imported once it has passed health checks at US borders, and the claims are therefore hard to substantiate. The US will not buy uncooked meat from Brazil, because of the foot-and-mouth disease in that country, so no Brazilian meat ends up in US hamburgers, though it can go elsewhere and still contribute largely to US foods such as corned beef.

Central America's hamburger forests

In Central America, the process of forest destruction is particularly complicated, with the hamburger coming relatively late, but crucially, into the picture. Two thirds of Central America's lowland and lower montane rainforest has been cleared since 1950, at a rate which continues at about 4,000 km² a year. First, logging companies go in for the wood (see **Cooking**), especially for valuable hardwoods such as mahogany and tropical cedar, which they often take out at unnecessarily great cost to the rest of the forest canopy.

Using the roads which the loggers create, land-starved peasants move in

Number of days protein supply for one person from one hectare	
Soybeans	5,495 days
Wheat	2,192 days
Corn	875 days
Used for beef	190 days

and complete the clearance, and plant mostly subsistence crops such as corn, beans and rice, with perhaps cash crops such as **coffee**, chillies, **bananas** and cacao. The logging and peasant farming activities take a big toll on the indigenous peoples, and in many cases hired guns have done deliberately what new diseases and competition for land have done by tragic accident.

The cleared land often falls prey to the ecological results of exploitative farming (declining soil fertility, disease probems, pests). The land is then ripe for purchase and aggregation into big units by entrepreneurial farmers who can afford pesticides and reseeding, especially since they are aided by government funding, whilst the peasant was not. In some Central American countries, the ranchers use the slash-and-burn techniques used in Brazil.

Cattle farmer in Namibia.

The Brazilian technique

During the 1960s and 1970s, the Brazilian authorities encouraged 'development' of their immense forest of millions of square kilometres. Large corporations and others bought land in the Amazonian rainforest at prices as low as $28 per hectare. By successively burning and reseeding fast-growing clump grass, in an attempt to keep the forest at bay whilst ranching beef at densities of 1 animal per hectare, a destructive cycle came about which, it is reckoned, will devastate the soil after 15 years.

Tropical forest soils are fragile. The forests hold most of their nutrients and minerals in the growing flora, rather than in the poor soils, whose productivity is quickly exhausted. In Brazil especially, the ranchers seldom attempt to make any use of the tropical woods they find. A vast conflagration puts an end to millenia of forest development in a few hours. Such farms employ very few people (see **Jobs**). They produce very little meat in comparison with their land-take, or with the way in which indigenous people use such land.

The cash crop problem

Though two thirds of Central America's arable land is now in beef production, beef consumption per capita in some Central American countries fell by a third during the 1970s, when beef production, mostly for export, more than doubled. This is the perennial problem with poor people who try to use their resources for profitable exchange with rich countries.

Feedlot hamburgers

Feedlots take young adult animals and fatten them – sometimes 200,000 at a time – in pens surrounding water, grain and forage supplies. It takes about 4,700 l of, often, and increasingly, very scarce water to produce 1 kg of beef. In eating 30 g of beef, an American uses more water than he or she draws from a tap daily. In a feedlot, about 50 kg of animal protein is produced for every 790 kg of plant protein fed to the beasts. About two thirds of US harvested land (excluding grazing rangeland) is used to feed animals, many of them in factory-style pens or sheds. If Americans halved their dependence on animal protein (to healthier levels), they would reduce agriculture's energy-take by 60%.

12 Eggs: nature's own pre-packed nutrition, but from cages

"The French, who are great egg-eaters, take singular pains as to the food of laying hens, in winter. They let them out very little, even in their fine climate, and give them very stimulating food: barley boiled, and given them warm; curds; buckwheat (which, I believe, is the best thing of all, except curds); parsley and other herbs chopped fine; leeks chopped in the same way; also apples and pears chopped very fine; oats and wheat cribbled; and sometimes they give them hemp-seed, and the seed of nettles; or dried nettles, harvested in summer, and boiled in winter."

William Cobbett *The Cottage Economy* (London, 1823)

THE modern, rich-world hen does not peck about in the yard, living on scraps. Nor does she, as her ancient predecessor did, live by pecking in fields amongst cattle, adding her bit of fertiliser to the fields and helping to keep them clean of pests.

Since the war, the farmyard hen has been banished to cages, usually stacked in tiers, while her day-old male offspring are more or less brutally slaughtered to provide pet food and soup. Even in the 1960s in the UK 50% of eggs came from the comparatively benign deep-litter system, but nearly a third still came from freerange systems. But now, 96% of eggs come from battery 'farms'.

Mercifully, it is now possible to buy freerange eggs at specialist shops and some supermarkets, and freerange egg production is now the only reliably profitable form of egg production. And though the freerange hen consumes far more feed than her caged sister, she can be fed a wider range of cheaper foods, is more valuable at the end of her laying life and provides more people with a living as they look after her and the rest of her flock.

One employee watches over 20,000 birds or more under intensive conditions, but only 2,000 under the freerange system. Yet, in a period of high unemployment in the rich world, the freerange system is none the less usually derided by official agricultural agencies. In the Third World, intensive systems are being widely promoted, in spite of their implications for lack of employment.

In the UK, egg consumption has risen from about 100 eggs per head per year at the turn of the century to around 250 now. In the USA, egg consumption was historically far higher per capita than in the UK (by one turn-of-the-century calculation, about 211 eggs per head per year). The USA produces around 65,000 million eggs a year, and the UK around 13,000 million. These figures amount to 280 (US) and 232 (UK) eggs per year per man, woman and child in the community. In the USA, egg per capita consumption has been falling: from an annual 335 in 1960, to about 270 in the early 1980s.

In the case of the US and the UK, both amongst the most intensive of egg producers, these figures mean that there is at least one battery hen (or a younger bird being grown ready for production) living her life in a cage for each of us. She will be a bird which is routinely dosed with antibiotics, enfeebled of wing and leg because of generations of breeding for productivity rather than well-being, and prone to mass nervous hysteria in the flock. In some flocks she will have had her beak cauterised in what is often a very painful operation, and be sent to her death after one or two years of laying.

She will also have gobbled up quantities of feed, whose sources will vary according to current world prices, and sometimes include a good deal of **fish**meal, rape seed and soya, much of which could be fed to humans. It was the trebling (and more) of feed prices during the early and mid-1970s that partly led to the intensification of hen farming. Whilst the price per egg had fallen in real terms by almost half in the post 1950s boom in intensification, it began rapidly to rise after successive increases in world oil prices, which dramatically affected feedstuff prices. The favourite route round expensive rich-world prices is to hunt for cheaply produced feedstuffs from the Third World, which of course increases the Third World dependence on feeding our animals instead of their humans (see **Livestock**).

Fossil energy kcal input/protein kcal output

	10	20	30	40	50	60	70	80	90
Milk									
Eggs									
Chicken									
Catfish									
Pork									
Beef (feedlot)									
Beef (rangeland)									
Lamb (rangeland)									

Index of efficiency: what fuel goes in – what food comes out. Units of fossil energy input per unit of protein energy output for various foods

Actually, of course, the contribution of eggs to the Western diet is doubly controversial. We have insisted on cheap food, and ignored the depredations of modern methods of farming on the animals involved (see

Milk). But we do not need cheap food in the rich world, since most of us are overfed and especially, in the view of many doctors, oversupplied with animal fats of exactly the kind eggs are rich in. We could spend our current household egg budget on buying fewer but more humanely produced eggs.

Across the very varied needs of different individuals in a population, the usual assumption is that an average of 2,500 calories per day per capita is adequate. However, in the USA, for instance, the average intake is one and half times this recognised requirement (which of course contributes to obesity), whilst in Zaire, the average intake is 17% below average requirement. The usual assumption about protein (the body-builder) is that, across the different individuals in a population, an average of about 55 g per day per capita is adequate. In the USA, however, the figure is nearly double the requirements, whilst in Zaire it is only a little over a half.

Although the US citizen could manage pretty well on his current vegetable intake alone, he takes in almost a further third of his actual protein from animal sources. However, his animal protein takes a far higher percentage of the land and energy needed for the US diet than does the vegetable portion. In Zaire, the average person takes only 60 calories a day in the form of animal products.

Freerange chickens in England – a relatively rare sight.

13 Milk: the breast and the udder

MILK, always imagined to be the most natural of foods, is actually increasingly a product which consumes vast quantities of energy and drugs in its making. Perhaps worse, it is associated with a good deal of animal suffering. The contented cow, docile in her field, is now no more than a convenient nursery-rhyme myth.

The world's production of milk has been rising steeply. There are at least 18 million more milking cows in the world than there were a decade ago, and they have boosted world production from 394,474,000 tonnes of milk to 437,909,000 tonnes. But although milk yields per animal have been rising worldwide, there remain vast differences in yield from country to country. Indian cows produce about half a tonne of milk a year per head, but in the USA each cow manages 10 times that amount, at well over 5.5 tonnes. The Japanese milk producer gets an average 4.6 tonnes of milk from each cow. The relatively 'inefficient' French farmer squeezes a little under 3.5 tonnes of milk from each of his animals, whilst the UK manages a little over 5 tonnes of milk per cow.

However, a country's contribution to world total production does not depend on yields per animal. France, with 10 million milking cows (1 for every 5 people in the population) produces more than twice as much milk as does the UK, with its far fewer but more productive cows. (The UK has 3.3 million cows – 1 for every 17 people). Russia is the greatest producer of milk in the world, followed by the US, whose 11 million cows (1 for every 230 people) only slightly outnumber their French cousins, but produce nearly twice as much total milk. Though the American milking-cow population fell by almost 2 million, or around 17%, between the late 1960s and now, total milk production rose by 17.5%.

The rush into high productivity – that is, high yields per cow – has become dizzying in the rich world particularly. Only Russia has contrived to reduce its yields per cow. Though Australia has made only modest gains in yield per animal, about 2% in the past decade, Japan (14.5%), Ireland (17%), US (18%), France (nearly 19%) and the UK (20%) have achieved an astonishing increase in yields in an industry which was already highly developed. In 1974, the UK cow was already giving a yield which was 16% up on a decade previously.

In many countries, notably in the US, Britain and France, milk subsidies have led farmers into producing milk using high levels of concentrated feeds. This overcomes the problem for the cow of absorbing huge inputs of energy through bulky forage materials such as grass. The cow is now fed grains, rather than grass; in some cases, she is 'zero-grazed', and never feeds on grassland pasture at all. But, partly because the fat content of milk and other dairy products has been associated with heart disease, there is a finite and often falling demand for a product which until only a few years ago was regarded as a great benefit to good health.

While Americans consume rather less dairy produce than they did in the 1950s, the average American cow now produces twice as much milk. Faced with a 5·9 billion kg surplus of dairy products, about 10% of total production in 1983, the American government had plans to pay farmers a bonus for reducing their milk production, just as previously they were given bonuses for increasing it.

In Britain, milk consumption is falling from nearly 2.8 l a week per person in the mid-1960s to nearer 2.3 l now, whilst in the USA it has fallen by nearly a third per capita, though in both countries other products, notably cheese and yoghurt, have shown increases.

As part of what is likely to be a continuing trend away from high subsidies to farmers, and in an attempt to reduce the massive milk 'lake' amongst its members, the European Community, in April 1984, announced a cutback in dairy subsidies, to be achieved by a quota system under which most dairy farmers have had to reduce production by 10%.

Poor cow

The better sort of American, Japanese or European cow produces around 10 times its own weight in milk every year. She does it, of course, as a result of producing a yearly calf, which is usually snatched from her within hours of birth, and often without its full quota of the chlostrum which its mother produces in her milk for a short period after giving birth, and which alone provides a calf with natural resistance to many diseases.

Such a calf will – unless it is in the small minority, and a splendid enough animal to become a future dairy cow or a fully fledged beef animal – be trucked, at a few days old, to a market. There it may or may not be sold and become pet food, pie or soup, or go into the veal trade. Although this trade is usually very cruel, this is not always and everywhere the case. Much British veal is now produced fairly humanely. If it is not sold, it may then be trucked to further markets, with an increasing toll in stress and illness, so that it is often routinely dosed with antibiotics to keep it in condition.

The cow herself will nowadays usually spend many hours on concrete and be amongst the quarter of cows every year with lameness problems. She will often suffer from ketosis, which occurs when an animal cannot efficiently turn her food into milk, and results in weight loss, infertility and general ill health. Ketosis is manageable with enough stockmanship skill and precise feeding, but it has been claimed that these are quite often absent on large dairy units, where the manpower per cow is half of what was available in less intensive days. It has been claimed that an extra well-trained farmworker working with a 100-cow herd would be worth at least 3 times his salary in increased production due to disease and illness control.

Mastitis, a disease of the udder, is on the increase on British farms, mostly because cowsheds are not as clean and sanitary as they were when there was more manpower and straw for good management of bedding. The disease runs at levels 3 times those expected in more traditional cow-keeping. Most cows are now treated routinely with antibiotics at the end of each lactation (the period during which they are in milk after calving), but the third of British cows which develop clinical mastitis during a lactation are then given further shots. These depredations on the cow are part of the reason that most cows are 'culled' after only 3 or 4 lactations, at 5, 6 or 7 years old, though in well-kept pedigree herds, cows often manage 14 lactations and upwards and seem in good health.

The cow as converter

The cow used to be an animal that took grazing grasses and some other green vegetables from the fields around it and converted them into milk. But in order to improve its yields, it has been increasingly fed on grains which are suitable for human consumption and which have a high fossil-energy input (see **Livestock**). Now, considerably less than half the plant protein which is fed to a New York State dairy cow is from grasses.

Though she is an efficient converter of plant protein (about a third of plant protein fed to her turns into protein in milk which humans can retrieve), in energy terms a cow is much less efficient. Of 30 units of food energy which are fed to her (increasingly in the form of energy derived from fossil fuel in the heavily fertilised grain), she can make only 1 unit of milk protein. Taking account of the fossil fuel required in tractors, trucks, manure-movers and so on, the energy-input/protein-output ratio falls to around 36:1.

Milk and vegetarianism

As we have seen, milk cannot be part of a properly vegetarian diet. Its inevitable by-product – a dead calf or beef animal, and, eventually, a dead cow, which was probably, with modern methods, an overstressed one – is deeply implicated in animal welfare. Beyond that, the energy implications of milk production place it firmly amongst the high-cost animal products, though it is nearly twice as efficient as feedlot **livestock** or **hamburgers**.

Roughly speaking, a pure vegetarian diet (sometimes known as vegan) is 3 times as energy efficient as a carnivorous diet, whilst the half-way stage (lacto-ovo vegetarianism, in which milk and eggs are consumed but not meat) consumes twice as much energy as a pure vegetarian menu. In some rich countries, notably the US, the intake of vegetables is increasing quite steadily, whilst the intake of meat products is beginning to fall overall.

Milk and the Third World

Though total milk production in developed countries has risen by about 9% in the last decade, the rise in total production in the developing world has been far higher, at 21%. But average yields in the poor world are a fifth of those in the rich world, and are rising more slowly. This is mostly because the poor world still grazes its cows rather than feeding them expensive grain.

Milk is a valuable food source provided it is produced on land which has few alternative uses. However, much Third-World milk is produced for people who are already well fed, and may take land away from purposes more useful to the poor. Moreover, much of the baby milk which is consumed in the Third World comes as a gift from rich countries keen to rid themselves of their surplus.

Many of these gift baby-milk powders are in practice made up with contaminated water, since few Third-World people can get a clean **glass of water**, or afford to sterilise unclean supplies by **cooking** them. Beyond that, they are often diluted to make them resemble mother's milk in appearance, or simply to stretch supplies. In some Third World cultures, women are prone to the view that well-promoted baby milk powders, and even evaporated milk, are better for their babies and growing children than mother's milk or, for older children, other cheaper sources of nourishment. This trend is much deplored by nutritionists because mother's milk is generally better than formulated milk and improved feeding of the mother is a better route to improving a baby's milk intake than giving it reconstituted cow's milk. Nutritionists point out that human mother's milk provides their babies with resistance to disease, whereas a cow's milk does not, being geared to provide resistance only for calves.

Though codes of practice have been accepted by many of the big milk formulators, following intense pressure from medical associations, they are widely regarded as inadequate, and unlikely to reverse the trend away from breast-feeding in poor countries.

Calves and petfood

The young calves which are taken from milk cows (and the chicks of hens, see **eggs**) are often used in petfood. An ordinary rich-world cat of around 4.5 kg-5.4 kg consumes about 250-300 calories a day, mostly in the form of animal products. That is getting on for double the animal product protein intake of the average African (177 calories per day) and well above that of the average Asian (200 calories per day). The average person in Zaire has around 60 calories a day in animal product form, about a fifth of that consumed by a rich-world cat.

The average rich-world cat consumes around $200 worth of food a year, more than the gross national product per capita of the 7 poorest nations on earth: Chad, Bangladesh, Ethiopia, Nepal, Mali, Burma and Zaire.

14 Fish: man's last hunted prey

THE rich world has turned its back on the vast majority of fish. Cod (to its particular peril), haddock and plaice now predominate as the species preferred. Since the early 1970s, total fish consumption in the Western world has been falling and frozen fish has been the only growth area. Frozen fish consumption in Britain, for instance, has risen by almost 50% in the last decade and a half, but we eat a third less fresh fish or even the ubiquitous fish with chips.

Seafood accounts, on world average, for around 6% of protein consumed by humans, and around 17% of animal protein. (Plants account for 65% of protein consumed by humans; meat for 16% and **milk** for nearly 10%.) But some countries – about 32 – take well over a third of their animal protein from seafood, and a further 11 take double the world average. The export business for seafood – excluding domestic consumption by fishing countries – runs at about $15,000 million, with Japan importing around a quarter of the total to support its 40 kg per capita annual fish consumption, itself around 4 times the global average of 11.6 kg.

Factory trawlers are now so large and efficient that some of them fish 10,000 tonnes a year, 10 or 20 times the catch of even a 50-footer. Fishing nations field huge fleets in competition with one another in an enterprise which can yield none of them sustainable profits. But fish catches could be increased dramatically if the fishing nations of the world could agree to apportion fish stocks amongst themselves. After a threefold growth in total catches since the Second World War, world fish catches are running at about 20 million tonnes less than might be the case if overfishing had not damaged fish populations so severely in the past.

At least 25 of the world's major fisheries have been damaged by over-fishing: high-tech ships and abuse of regulations have seen to that. In the North Atlantic, cod populations were so damaged in the 1960s that they are now a third of what they might have been. Between 1975 and 1980 cod catches were halved in the North Atlantic. In the same period, North Sea herring catches fell from 3.7 million tonnes to well under 0.75 million tonnes, whilst pilchard catches off south west Africa fell from 1 million tonnes to 12,000 tonnes.

Big ships are now searching the oceans for the few species of fish which man finds attractive (predominately white fish), often overfishing the stocks they find. In the North Sea, the herring industry virtually collapsed in the late 1970s when governments were unable to reach agreement on a co-operative reduction in catches, in line with scientific advice which had been well advertised to them.

It is mostly developed nations and their fishermen who have over-exploited their fisheries, Peru and Chile being lone Third Worlders in a list which includes Japan, the USSR, France and South Africa. Putting fishing into the hands of nations which need it for their peoples' dietary well-being is one of the great development issues facing the world.

The fishing industry is hugely wastful. Not less than three tonnes of fish are thrown away dead by shrimp fishermen for every tonne of their target catch. Every year 20,000 porpoises fall victim to salmon gill-netters in the north Atlantic and north Pacific. Tens of thousands of dolphins are killed annually by tuna fishermen, though this incidental take could be sharply reduced. Sometimes, as in the case of young halibut trawled by mistake, the 'trash' fish are vital to the recovery of fisheries.

How our fish catch is used (as a percentage of total world fish haul)	
For human consumption	**70%**
Marketing fresh	*30%*
Freezing	*18%*
Curing	*12%*
Canning	*10%*
For other uses (oils and meals)	**30%**

Energy expense

Fishing off the US coast routinely uses 4 times more fossil energy (measured in kilo calories) than can be returned in protein calories, an energy expense several times that obtained from fish catches nearer to coasts. The reasons for this are partly that big ships are less efficient than small ships; partly that big ships are used to travel larger distances for their catches; and partly that inshore fish tend to be zoo-plankton eaters, and therefore efficient storers of energy, whilst the deep-sea fish (so hard sought) are carnivorous hunters, several links up the food chain, which are less good at storing food energy for our use. Up to a half of the running costs of a deep-sea trawler are for fuel, approximately half of which is used to power the ship, and half for the fridges.

Almost all creatures, including man, live by the results of photosynthesis. The only exceptions are some creatures living in the mineral-rich and warm volcanic deepwater sites in the Pacific. Our harvest of the sunlight which falls on the earth and its oceans is gathered with greatest efficiency if we eat vegetable products, and diminishes as we eat those vegetables after they have been processed through the digestive systems of other creatures. (See **Livestock**. Much fish is processed as cattle feed.)

Each link in the food chain passes on as available energy 10% of what it has consumed. This rule is very rough, and is known as 'Lindeman's Ten Per Cent Law', after the young American ecologist who first promulgated the notion in the 1950s. The predator deep-ocean fish have therefore been part of a series of predations which leaves the final consumer with a very low proportion of the energy which went into their creation. What is worse, much industrial fishing for species used in fishmeal for cattle takes an accidental catch of young fish which, had they been allowed to survive, would have grown to a crop worth far more than the fishmeal harvest in which they were accidentally killed.

Even small inshore fishing boats use about twice as much fossil energy as their catches return in protein energy, though fuel constitutes only 15% of their running costs. But ocean-going, deep-sea fishing ships routinely turn in energy expenditures 10 times as profligate: 21 kcal of energy per kcal of fish protein harvested. In the American fishing industry overall, 27 kcal of fossil

Index of efficiency: what fuel goes in – what food comes out. Units of fossil energy input per unit of protein energy output for various foods.

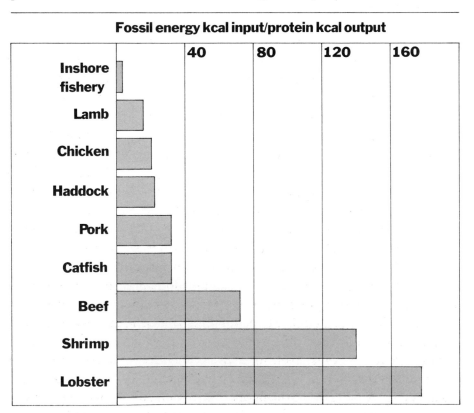

Fossil energy kcal input/protein kcal output

	40	80	120	160
Inshore fishery				
Lamb				
Chicken				
Haddock				
Pork				
Catfish				
Beef				
Shrimp				
Lobster				

energy are expended for each kcal of fish protein. Herring needs only 2 units of fossil energy for each unit of protein energy, whilst cod needs 20 units. The cropping of lobster, a luxury species, is a further 10 times more extravagant, at neary 200 kcal expended for every kcal of lobster protein. None the less, it takes only a tenth of the energy to power a trawler to catch and deliver 1 kg of cod as it does to produce the soyabean meal which might be fed to a steer (see **Hamburgers**) to produce 1 kg of meat.

Anchovies are expensively fished off Peru mostly for their value as cattle feed. When fed to animals, the fish lose nine tenths of their nutritional potential. The north-eastern seaboard of the US provides fish for direct human consumption 6 times more efficiently than the Peruvian anchovy grounds provide fish which are fed to animals. The peculiarity of these relative inefficiencies would not matter so much if fossil energy was endlessly and equitably available, but it is not. It is the capacity of rich nations to buy fossil fuels which most marks them out from poor nations. Using their hold on expensive fuels, the rich countries go into the world's oceans and deplete their stocks of fish in a harvest which is mostly squandered by being fed to non-human animals.

Pilchards

Jenny Amery, a worker for the Catholic Institute for International Relations, reported in 1983 that women at the Peruvian fishing town of Chimbote were paying an extraordinary human price in providing the housewives of rich countries with tinned pilchards for their suppers and for those of their cats. The town's 30 factories can produce 3 million cans a day, three quarters of which are exported to the supermarkets of the West, often under familiar names. Although the town's population has grown from 5,000 inhabitants before the war, to its present 300,000, the canning plants depend on cheap female labour. The average wage for a 16-hour shift is $1, and the women are reportedly forbidden to leave the factory whilst waiting for a fish catch to arrive, though they are not paid for their waiting time. Sometimes they work with spicy sauce fillings which burn their hands so much that only a prolonged soaking in iced water will aid the inflamation.

Jenny Amery reported at least one amputation after a fish-spine wound turned septic; the injured party received no compensation from the company. The woman work with hands immersed in freezing water and fish entrails and are often soaked from head to foot, but the companies do not provide gloves or boots. Even so, there is an almost limitless demand for work since the town has become a magnet for people desperate to leave the countryside; 70% of the townspeople have no regular work, and 75% of them live in shanty towns, often without sanitation (see **Glass of Water**).

Fish farming

We now, as a species, no longer hunt for our food, but farm it instead. Around the world the practice of fish farming is increasing at the rate of about 5% a year as the Occident rediscovers skills which were once common. At present, 9 million tonnes of fish are, if not domesticated, at least managed for maximum yield, during some or all of their lives, in millions of hectares of ponds, paddies and fish ranches.

In China, 40% to 50% – approximately 4 million tonnes – of the fish eaten has been farmed in about 10 million hectares of land covered by fish farms, often as an integral part of the 40 million hectares of irrigated land in China. Chinese production is often almost incredibly efficient, at 3-5 tonnes of fish per hectare per year. There, as elsewhere in Asia, some farms are fed by piggeries built directly over the water so that manure falls onto the fish. Chinese fish constitutes about half the total of world farmed fish; the rest of Asia provides a further 1.5 million tonnes, whilst in Africa the practice is in its infancy.

Fish farming and pesticides

In parts of the East, fish and paddy farming have co-existed for many years. However, changes in irrigation practices (see **Irrigation**) and especially in rice production have complicated this union. In Sri Lanka, for example, several species of fish which lived in the ditches, paddies and reservoirs were useful contributors to the peasant diet; often these are now killed by pesticides. These fish were also good predators of mosquito larvae and their death has resulted in an increasing incidence of malaria, which 200 million people round the world suffer from at any one time (see **Glass of Water**). The disease has singularly outwitted the pesticide campaign waged against it with some success a decade or so ago.

So profound is the ignorance about pesticides in some Ghanaian villages that they often poison their fish for consumption in preference to normal netting or hooking. People complain of dizziness and worse, but do not make the connection between the poisoned fish and their own illness.

In Indonesia, where fish farming in rice fields produces about a quarter of all inland fresh-fish production, and fish makes up about two thirds of animal protein consumed, pesticide poisoning in paddies is very dangerous. Since rice farmers not only wash and wade in the paddy water, but also eat cattle and fowl which drink and fish which live in the paddy's waters, their pollution by pesticides is very hazardous indeed. Moreover, the green revolution species of rice require a lower level of water, which reduces the paddy's value as a fish farm.

The partly good news

Jesus made a few fishes feed the five thousand; modern man has succeeded in reversing the formula. We now crop a huge quantity of fish and eat surprisingly little of it directly. On the seven tenths of the planet which is ocean, we now hunt down around 76 million tonnes of fish with an efficiency which no non-human animal hunter could manage. We hunt some of them, including the most valuable of the species, beyond the capacity of their populations to sustain overall numbers. We do it with an energy expenditure which wastes the world's fuel resources in shocking disproportion to the crop's capacity to fuel us, whilst doubly squandering even such huge energy expenditures by feeding fish to other animals which we then kill for food. Consumed directly, the fish would provide us with double their present energy.

None the less, there is speculation that modest investment ($1.5 billion annually) could double world fish catches in a couple of decades. Useful targets would be the south-west Atlantic and the Indian oceans, where no new technology would be required to exploit at least a further 2 million tonnes of valuable white fish.

15 Drugs: the most dangerous cash crop

Drug use, especially of the 'soft' kind, is 'normal' all over the rich world, and increasingly also in parts of the poor world. In America, 25 million people use marijuana occasionally and around 50 million are reckoned to have tried it at some time; some 17 million have essayed cocaine and 5 million use it regularly (contributing to the 122 cocaine-related deaths in the US in 1981). Of the 4 million Americans who sometimes take heroin, 500,000 are addicted. The fact that only a quarter of the heroin users are addicted supports the assertion of some heroin users and fans that it can be a controlled habit. However, it matters a great deal that it might take death to discover whether one is amongst the lucky 1 in 4 'fun'-users.

The illegality of drugs makes those who use or abuse them criminals automatically. This increases the expensiveness of the habit and thus creates further criminals amongst users; and it creates the profits which make drugs a rich racket for organised crime rather than for the organised taxation which would almost certainly thrive on them otherwise.

In many American states (and often in practice in Britain too), the possession and smoking of marijuana is only formally a crime: first offenders are automatically given conditional discharges. In Britain, however, many people of Afro-Caribbean origin believe that their widespread habit of smoking marijuana gives the police an open invitation to stop and search members of their community.

The normalisation of drug taking means that hardly any modern adult does not know of a friend with a son or daughter who is an addict. Cheaper supplies of heroin have made it all too common. In one big Edinburgh housing estate perhaps 1 in 12 of the youngsters is using heroin, and three quarters of house break-ins are drugs-related.

Some authorities reckon that in cosmopolitan districts, 1 in 50 young adults may be a heroin user. There are probably 50,000 regular heroin users in Britain today, a doubling in a very few years, and production of the drug has spread to countries such as Pakistan, where it was virtually unknown a decade ago. Heroin seizures in Britain by the customs authorities are running at 3 times their 1980 levels, and are now worth nearly $34.5 million at street prices.

"In Bhutan, marijhuana is fed to the pigs, not the people. 'This makes the pigs happy, and us happy,' says the foreign minister."

Quoted by Geoffrey Lean, the *Observer Magazine*, 18 November 1984

There may be 300,000 heroin users in Poland, with a rather high percentage of them being addicts. Some of the country's peasants have found growing poppies rather more lucrative than bothering with food.

In Britain there has been a recent and continuing epidemic in the tragic and mostly teenage habit of glue (solvent) sniffing, which has caused 100 deaths in the last couple of years.

Growing drugs ... in California

The publicly owned forests of north California are widely used for the illicit marijuana crop, of which some $250 million worth was seized in that state during 1981 alone. Both at home and abroad, the US government occasionally embarks on spraying programmes to render the marijuana plants unusable or kill them.

There has long been controversy over the US government's attempts to spray marijuana crops in the US and in Colombia, Jamaica and Mexico, where several sprayers have been shot by growers over the years. The crops are sprayed with the pesticide paraquat (known as 'liquid machete'), which can now be 'signalled' with a chemical known as 'essence of skunk' which warns smokers of the dangerous contamination by chemicals when they light up their spliff (joint, cigarette).

At first, spraying abroad merely boosted home production, in spite of stiff penalties, and chemical companies themselves refused to co-operate with the programme since they feared being sued by damaged users. The US courts overruled their objections.

Marijuana is huge business. It is America's second most valuable crop (after wheat) and well over 1 million people grow $16.6 billion's worth, an eighth of it in California alone. Marijuana sales in the US are said to come close to rivalling those of the legal cigarette business, and are perhaps twice those of the beer business.

... and Colombia and Bolivia ...

In many other countries, such as Colombia, marijuana production was just another cash crop to threaten what have for centuries been stable, though very poor, agricultural communities. More recently, with US home production of marijuana high, South America has turned increasingly to harder drugs.

Bolivia now depends crucially for its income on the drug trade which is worth $2 billion in cocaine alone. This represents 30% of its export earnings and is worth more than its foreign tin sales. Much of it is routed through Colombia. One of the main supply routes out of the Andes is a track originally built by the Americans to help open a new wheat-field area.

Instead, it helps provide America with half the US cocaine imports, reckoned to total 67 tonnes in 1982.

In the jungles of Bolivia, and especially in the Chapare region, whose clearings once grew pineapples, **coffee, sugar** cane and rice, the coca bush – once grown only as a subsistence crop – now dominates. (A detoxified resin from its leaves is still used in Coca-Cola (see **Soft Drinks**) as indeed a toxic component once was.) An American satellite survey suggests that Chapare alone could be producing 50,000 tonnes of coca leaf, which may produce up to 180 tonnes of the cocaine people buy on the street.

The paraffin, lime and acid treatments which extract the coca leaf's cocaine alkaloids add big profits for the producers who buy from the growers. Even so, a further 600% profit is available for those dealers who buy

A bushman woman enjoys a smoke.

from the producers and sell into the rich world. At various times Bolivian government officials and armed services have been deeply involved in the trade, sometimes by controlling it, but always using it as a rich source of back-handers. Peculiar muddle, then, obtains where a country's foreign earnings mostly depend on a wholly illegal trade which provides farmers with their only half-way profitable cash crop and makes individuals in the government and services rich. The only people who seem to get caught are the occasional relatively lowly traffickers who rot in gaol whilst the big-timers run free.

Columbia is a major centre for cocaine production, though increasingly the country's peasants turn to growing the raw commodity, coca. In March 1984, the brave Señor Rodrigo Lara, Columbia's justice minister, organised a raid on a cocaine-producing plant deep in the jungle. This was part of his crackdown on the drugs trade, which was already identifying senior businessmen and politicians who were implicated. The production plant was heavily defended by guerrillas (who are in protection rackets), but was shut down, and cocaine with a street value of $1.2 billion was seized. The raid cost Señor Lara his life: he was gunned down in April as he returned home in his chauffeur-driven Mercedes.

But the raid also sparked off a resurgence of guerrilla actions which led to President Betancur's having to withdraw, in some regions of his country, the amnesty he had been offering to guerrillas. In July, there was even a secret meeting between government ministers and some of the racketeers who had fled. They offered to shut down their operations in exchange for an amnesty against extradition orders to the US. This was refused them, having been roundly condemned on all sides as grotesque. In November 1984 there was a bomb explosion outside the American embassy in Bogota, killing a Columbian passer-by. As a result, the president of Columbia was reported to be in favour of extradition arrangements between the US and this country – a first step in limiting the drugs trade.

... and Peru ...

The US effort to slow down cocaine production in Peru was severely damaged in 1984 when 21 members of an anti-cocaine squad were massacred in Tingo Maria, on the main tributary of the upper Amazon.

... and Asia ...

It was Chaing Kai-shek's supporters, on the run from Mao's revolutionary victories in 1949, who first introduced commercial development of the opium crop to the Thai-Burmese-Laotian border region now known as the Golden Triangle. They also brought the scientific knowledge to turn opium into heroin. Now, various sincere and serious separatist groups use the opium trade as a means of financing their fight against the Burmese government and its troops.

In recent years, however, especially since crackdowns by the Thai government, the 'Golden Crescent' on the frontiers of Iran, Afghanistan and Pakistan began dramatically to increase its share of the market (though the Golden Triangle warlords seem to have stepped up their production again recently). Now, in what seems to be a traditional phenomenon, Afghan refugees in the border country make their living from growing poppies, and some of the income from the trade goes into supporting the rebel cause against the Russian invaders.

This new producing region meant that Pakistani traders had large quantities of heroin to sell and were often prepared to sell it more cheaply than marijuana. Turkish dealers are also trading strongly in some countries. They have all been contributing to massive inflows of relatively cheap and pure heroin which began with the fall of the Shah, when many fleeing exiles brought their wealth westwards in the form of the drug.

... and Australia

Marijuana is the third most valuable cash crop in Australia. Griffith in New South Wales is reputed to be the main headquarters of the drugs business, which is controlled by families which originated in, and still deal with, Mafia-dominated Calabria, in Italy. It is an irrigated vegetable-growing area, and thus has good transport links to major cities. One small Italian village, Plati, has more of its sons and daughters in Griffith than at home. Plati also has a fearsome reputation as a centre for kidnap operations, many of whose profits are believed to have funded the growing and trading of drugs in Australia. In Griffith in the 1970s, dirt farmers suddenly started building vast bungalows, known locally as 'grass castles'. A local politician and shop-owner was murdered for his crusade against the local drug trade.

16 Cigarettes: finding new people to give cancer to

SMOKING cigarettes has had a meteoric career as a profitable and dangerous enterprise whose major beneficiaries are governments, which raise revenue through taxes, and the companies that conduct this trade in narcotics. The two are at constant war as to what public policy should be. Governments, having to pay many of the costs of their citizens' addiction in medical expenses, are aware of an obligation to try to discourage the habit, while the companies note their tax contribution (as do the governments) and the needs of their workers for jobs.

And so, the world grows about 5.5 million tonnes of tobacco, nearly 65% of it in developing countries which do not benefit from the manufacturing side of the export business. All this in large part to feed a habit which has, in Europe, seen a colossal increase from its small commercial beginnings in the nineteenth century. In 1880 there was hardly any cigarette smoking, but in Britain alone by 1920, 36,000 million cigarettes were smoked annually, and 113,000 million by 1961. Consumption peaked at about 140,000 million in the 1970s and is now, following evidence of close correlations between smoking and disease, in decline, with sales of around 101,000 million in 1982. The tobacco industry now wonders if its sales have discovered their long-term low, or will continue to fall, as some health economists believe likely.

American cigarette sales have, in spite of health anxieties, increased steadily and are far and away the dominant form of tobacco consumption, accounting for 92% consumption of the leaf, as against less than 4% in 1900. American cigarette smokers puff their way through well over 600 billion weeds a.year. Tobacco products cost the US 1% of total disposable personal income, and the industry lobbyists are said to be able effectively to nobble any proposed government legislation against them.

Exporting the killer habit

Anxious that their domestic markets may well shrink dramatically over the next few years, cigarette companies have not only diversified into food, insurance, oil and shipping, but they have also made the controversial move (as have pesticide makers facing similar difficulties – see **Jeans**) of promoting sales of their products abroad. Whilst one study showed that only 7% of an American university's students smoked, a comparable figure for Nigeria was 10 times that proportion. In the decade to 1981, Africa's population increased its smoking consumption per capita by a third. In the decade to 1976, cigarette smoking doubled in Ethiopia and Libya.

The World Health Organisation believes that, as a result, a new rash of epidemics is likely to hit the Third World, where half the tobacco grown is kept for domestic consumption. Increases in incidence of cancer, emphysema and heat disease seem to follow a rise in cigarette smoking, and whilst people may be freed by expensive modern medicine to survive diseases 'indigenous' to their countries, they probably now risk sacrificing that benefit by importing new forms of disease.

A new use for the weed?

There is some hope that the tobacco plant's remarkable properties as a provider of protein of exceptional quality and all the amino acids needed by man may rescue the growers. This crop can be harvested on a cut-and-come-again basis and high yields have been proven. Tobacco may yet lose its association with smoking, and it will need to if consumers are to accept it as a food additive.

Japanese researchers have found that, ironically, tobacco may contain an anti-cancer ingredient, which – if isolated – may prove very useful.

Getting the East hooked on Western habits

Attempting to expand their fortunes and secure them against any future decline, American companies in particular have been trying to expand their business in Japan. There the per capita cigarette consumption is well over an annual 2,500, as against the US per capita consumption of 2,900, or, for the 54 million smokers, an average of 30 per day, over 11,000 per year.

The task will not be easy since protectionist Japan has a state-run tobacco and salt monopoly, which contributes annually around $7 billion, or half the retail price of cigarettes, in taxes. The government will be loath to allow its citizen-customers to indulge their taste for Americanisation. The Japanese know all about preserving home markets, and tobacco is a particularly sensitive industry for them since they produce cigarettes in inefficient plants and protect their tobacco growers by paying them around 3 times the world price for their crops.

Smoking and women

Elsewhere, there is a third world within a first world: women in rich countries are being treated to a marketing operation aimed at accelerating their rising demand for cigarettes. Certainly, in Britain between 1950 and 1975, the percentage of women who smoked rose from 38 to 43, whilst cigarette smokers amongst men declined from 62% to 47%. In more recent years the percentage of either men or women who smoke has been falling: 38% of men smoke, 33% of women. Women smokers tend to smoke slightly fewer cigarettes per week than their male counterparts. However, the average female smoker is now smoking twice as many cigarettes as was the average in 1950s, an average of 100 per week now. Respiratory cancer deaths have trebled from less than 1 per 10,000 of all women to nearer 3.

Smoking costs and benefits

Tobacco smoking is believed to kill about 50,000 (but perhaps 100,000) people a year in Britain, and that has been part of the moral rationale that allows governments to impose high taxes on its consumption. Currently, upwards of 70% of the retail price goes in taxation in Western countries in a range which begins at 60% in Greece and peaks with Denmark's 83%. UK smokers contribute upwards of $4,600 million a year to the treasury.

In Britain, the tobacco companies contribute to a $3.5 million fund, about 3% on top of their advertising budget, which is charged with researching better health. However, this money may specifically not be spent on tobacco-related problems, though they are probably the country's single biggest cause of ill-health, costing 50 million lost days and $172.5 million in medical treatment costs. In America, smoking, which has been officially designated as 'the chief preventable cause of death', has been estimated to cost $40 billion a year in lost time and medical costs.

The degree of health risk associated with smoking has now been reflected in cheaper insurance schemes for non-smokers. In America a survey in the early 1980s found that a average man of 32 who did not smoke could expect to live to be 79, whilst an average smoker of that age would not be likely to live beyond 72. Smokers are twice as likely to drop dead at any age than non-smokers. These figures have encouraged a rash of cheaper US and UK insurance for non-smokers.

In the UK every price incease which a new budget brings walks a tightrope between increased revenue on reduced sales and, at last, a loss in revenue concomitant on a severe loss in sales. Even tobacco addicts will not provide an endlessly price-elastic demand. None the less, between them, increased taxes and increased health worries spell bad news for tobacco workers. The industry employed 421,000 people in 1974, but by 1980, 6,000 jobs had gone, and a further 5,000 by 1983. Some British tobacco firms have been losing up to 15% of their jobs in recent years.

In the US there has not been an increase in cigarette tax for 30 years. Increasing the tax would have the merit of going some way to discourage smoking. Typically of new legal practices, the US has seen lawyers arguing that consumers should be able to sue tobacco firms for damage to health caused by their products. Lobbyists have named 45,000 studies identifying smoking as dangerous, addictive and often fatal (about 350,000 smoking-related premature deaths in the US annually).

Subsidising the killer in the EEC? Tobacco harvest in the Dordogne, France.

Subsidising the killer

Meanwhile, whilst the US government has warnings printed on cigarette packets, it also provides price support (and quotas) for American tobacco growers to grow their product at a price which makes it uncompetitive on the world market. Many of the growers in the States are poor farmers with small patches of land which they farm with high labour input. This is not the kind of farm operation which could easily be switched to other products.

In the European Community the agricultural policy designed to help poor farmers has had the odd effect of ensuring that the tax-payer pays for the tobacco for about 6 cigarettes in a packet of 20. Around half the tobacco smoked in the EEC has been grown there, and subsidised by the community to the tune of $663 million a year. About 60% of the costs to farmers of growing tobacco in the European community comes from Common Market funds. Around a quarter of a million farmers grow tobacco in the EEC, often on smallholdings of less than 1 hectare. Of the Greek population, 6% is involved in tobacco growing, and the country is the tenth largest exporter in the world. Spain and Portugal's membership of the EEC will add to the cost of subsidising French, Greek and Italian farmers who already grow the drug.

The environment and tobacco

Tobacco is demanding of nutrients, and this requires what are often unaffordable inputs of fertiliser if it is not hopelessly to degrade the soils in which it is grown. It is also a heavy user of pesticides, many of which are types sold in the Third World but banned or severely restricted in the rich world (see **Jeans**).

Aldrin is widely used, in for instance Kenya, and although it is supplied with instructions in several local languages, many of its users cannot read and certainly cannot quickly consult a doctor, as they are advised to do in case of accident.

Amongst the most pernicious effects of the tobacco business in the Third World is the deforestation which takes place as people burn wood to cure tobacco. Around half the tobacco grown in the world is flue-cured over wood fires.

At a rough estimate, something over 1 million hectares of open forest are stripped for this purpose worldwide, amounting to a tree for every 300 cigarettes produced in the Third World. As in the case of wood used for **cooking**, farmers are having to travel further and further afield to find wood supplies. To ensure a stable supply of the fuel needed for tobacco-curing, over 8 million hectares of afforestation would be needed: clearly, it will not happen. Another useful route might be to improve the efficiency of tobacco curing: over 80% of the fuel used is wasted in the process.

Smoking and growing in Bangladesh

In Bangladesh, the area of tobacco growing has been increasing rapidly: it stood at around 55,000 hectares in 1982, up from 47,000 in 1976. Tobacco smoking in this, one of the poorest nations on earth, has doubled in the past couple of decades. In the poor world in general, smoking is increasing far faster than population growth. Between 65% and 90% of the household

Depletion of soil nutrients by tobacco and other crops (loss in kg/ha)

Harvest of one mt per ha	Nitrogen N	Phosphorus P_2O_5	Potassium K_2O
Tobacco	**24.4**	**14.4**	**46.4**
Coffee	**15.0**	**2.5**	**19.5**
Maize	**9.8**	**1.9**	**6.7**
Cassava	**2.2**	**0.4**	**1.9**

expenditure of the poor and poorest households in Bangladesh goes on food and any increased take for smoking is likely therefore to affect food consumption. Smoking is mostly a male preserve in Bangladesh, and there is a strong presumption that as it increases amongst household heads, the children will be the ones whose food consumption suffers as a result.

In a 1981 study by health researcher Nicholas Cohen, an attempt was made to chart the impact of Bangladesh's smoking and tobacco growing on food consumption. He noted that the landowners were able to earn twice as much on their labour cost on land which was used for tobacco as against that used for rice, the staple. A Bangladeshi landworker might receive about the cash equivalent of 2 kg of rice for a day's work, or about enough for the energy requirement of a 12 kg child for a week.

But tobacco as a crop employs rather fewer local villagers than does rice, from which women, for instance, can earn a vital part of the family's livelihood in processing work.

Tobacco smoking in Bangladesh amounts to a business in which men switch their expenditure from food for their families in favour of a killing dependence on a drug which is itself grown in a way useful to the landowners but not the peasants.

The partly good news

In recent years there has been an interesting movement towards stressing the broader responsibilities of firms and their investors in the human and environmental effects of their operations. Often this movement has to work outside the conventional establishment, so it was doubly heartening when the British Medical Association (BMA) decided to publish the *Report on Investment in the UK Tobacco Industry* (London, 1985) which had been produced by a research and propaganda group, Social Audit.

The Report showed that many charities, including child welfare bodies and even some whose function was to promote good health, had investments in the tobacco industry. The publication was sponsored by the BMA, 'so that those who may have unwittingly invested in the tobacco industry can be so informed'. It highlights the difficulties in taking any sort of moral view of shareholdings in large firms, in which unpalatable operations may not be obvious. For instance, the hotel chain, Grand Metropolitan, also has an annual $575 million turnover, 10% of its total, in tobacco interests. The British Heart Foundation was none the less reported to have holdings in Grand Met.

17 **Packaging:** the throwaway mountain

THE average American, in his industry, household and institutions, is responsible for well over a tonne of waste per year. Most of it is disposed of into the 200,000 hectares of landfill dumps which litter the American landscape (this figure excludes mining waste, demolition rubble and junked cars). The most visible, and potentially most avoidable, tip of this junkberg is composed of packaging. The individual US citizen's annual food packaging accounts for 26 kg of paper, 36 kg of glass, 18 kg of steel, 3.6 kg of **aluminium** and 2.7 kg of plastic. His beer and **soft drinks** account for 19.5 kg of glass, 7.25 kg of steel and 1.8 lbs of aluminium.

About a third of the weight of municipal solid waste content is packaging materials, but very much more than that by bulk since packaging materials are mostly light and bulky. This makes them expensive to collect from the places they are junked in. A further 20% of the weight in a domestic dustbin is reading material.

One trip wonders

The US used 24 billion aluminium cans a year by the late 1970s. Of those, 18 million made 1 trip from bauxite mine to rubbish tip, with a probable period of a very few minutes of their life actually in their users' hands. Though much aluminium packaging is recycled (in some American states, such as California, around a quarter), and though in many countries some bottles are reused, especially in Britain those used for milk, most are neither reused nor recycled.

Poor societies do, of course, reuse many of their containers, simply because their components have value for refuse scavengers. Cairo's scavengers, for instance, collect about 2,000 tonnes of paper a month, which makes around 1,500 tonnes of recycled paper and cardboard.

The partly good news

In the rich world, there is a conscious movement by enlightened consumers and adventurous entrepreneurs toward reuse or recycling. However, this process has often been thwarted by the container manufacturers who routinely spend large sums in combating, for instance, legislation which aims at a compulsory deposit system. Such a system would make it worthwhile either for the original consumer or a scavenger to see the container returned to use rather than dumped.

Recycling aluminium is clearly useful since it requires only 4% of the energy to melt and recreate a given weight of aluminium in a recycling process, as against starting from scratch with smelting bauxite. It has been suggested that if bottle bills, which usually cover every sort of beverage container, were introduced nationally in the US, 500,000 tonnes of aluminium, 1.5 million tonnes of steel and 5.2 million tonnes of glass could be saved from the nation's landfill tips. This would also save around 46 million barrels of oil, in spite of the extra trips many empty containers would make back to the fillers.

Recycling versus reuse

Oddly enough, the glass industry, especially in Britain, has been at pains to promote the recycling (breaking up and remelting) of glass bottles, which are not ideal for that process since only about 8% energy savings can be made in recycling glass as against creating it fresh from silica. Glass bottles are thus ideal candidates, not for recycling, but for reuse.

Plastic has been much abused as an environmentally disastrous material for packaging, because it is virtually indestructible, often bobbing for years, for instance, around the oceans of the world. However, the material is now potentially ideal, provided that its permanence is used in the environment's favour and containers made from it are reused.

About 60 million tonnes of plastics are made worldwide, and in the US synthetic material production takes about 3% of the country's oil and natural gas consumption, although plastics makers are increasingly efficient in their use of petrol and gas.

A large proportion of plastics are used in packaging: in the US about a quarter, and worldwide about a sixth.

Though we usually think of petrol and gas as providing fuel for heat and transport, the take of energy for the production of synthetics (plastics and textiles combined) is such that the world's transport fleet would only have to achieve a third of a kilometre per litre increase in efficiency to yield enough naphtha to boost synthetics production by 50%.

Contrary to much received prejudice, and even though plastic containers lock up a good deal of energy compared with steel and even aluminium cans,

Package	kcal
Wooden berry basket	**69**
Styrofoam tray (size 6)	**215**
Moulded paper tray (size 6)	**384**
Polyethylene pouch (16 oz or 455 g)	**559**
Steel can, aluminium top (12 oz)	**568**
Small paper set-up box	**722**
Steel can, steel top (16 oz)	**1006**
Glass jar (16 oz)	**1023**
Coca Cola bottle, non-returnable (16 oz)	**1471**
Aluminium TV dinner container	**1496**
Aluminium can, pop-top (12 oz)	**1643**
Plastic milk container, disposable (½ gal)	**2159**
Coca Cola bottle, returnable (16 oz)	**2451**
Polyethylene bottle (1 qt)	**2494**
Polypropylene bottle (1 qt)	**2752**
Glass milk container returnable (½ gal)	**4455**

Fossil energy required to
produce various food
packages.

they do have a powerful – and, so far, largely hypothetical – potential for reuse, as against the known difficulty of recycling them.

It's up to us

Neither reuse nor recycling are easy. They depend on processes which are messy and time consuming, and are much more comfortably achieved in a populace which is willing. In rich countries, for instance, we usually discard **egg** cartons after one use. It is perfectly easy to take the 'empties' back to the shop for refilling, but hardly anyone does so (though in country districts in France this is certainly *de rigeur*). Beyond getting containers such as bottles back to shops for refilling (and in many cases that would involve a major change of heart, especially on the part of labour- and space-conscious supermarkets and their suppliers), it is important that waste be kept separate at its source. Paper, household food wastes, bottles, cans and plastic squeezies slammed together in the bin make an unholy mess which is very expensive to disentangle at the recycling plant. What poverty makes poor countries do – value their resources too much to use them only once – rich countries must learn to do as a matter of ecological good sense.

18 Jeans: cotton and pesticides for the image-conscious

EVERY pair of jeans represents between half and three quarters of 1 kg of cotton fabric, out of a total world cotton production of around 13 million tonnes annually. But the growing of the cotton earns a little less than a tenth of the price of the finished product. The distribution from the manufacturer of the jeans to the consumer takes up to half the total price.

Cotton has always been, and remains, a difficult crop to grow successfully. None the less, about 30 million hectares of land around the world are growing cotton: half of the total area which grows non-food crops. It provides around 40% of all the world's fibre, even including man-made fibres. Around 5% of the world's cultivated land is down to cotton, much of it land which once provided livelihoods for peasants, but which is now owned by local elites. Though cotton employs many people, its requirements are highly seasonal, which disrupts the lives of the workers. In many regions, irrigation has been provided for this high-profit crop, but water, fertiliser run-offs and pesticides make a dangerous environmental cocktail for the locals.

Cotton is prey to many pests and exhausts soils dangerously, having a high demand for nitrogen. This is one of the reasons why it is often grown in rotation with the **peanut,** which fixes nitrogen from the atmosphere.

The rise of King Cotton

The fibre had been known for centuries in countries such as Egypt. It became the King Cotton of the industrial revolution in northern Europe and the USA as soon as the machine revolution of the early nineteenth century removed garment manufacture from the growing regions.

As a crop requiring large quantities of labour, it was grown in the colonies of European countries (in India especially), or by slave labour in the States, which amounted economically to the same thing. Immigrant labour, from rural Europe in the case of the US, and from rural Britain in the case of the towns and cities of Britain's north-west, came to the factories where cotton could be made into cloth.

The Southern states of the US only started making the cloth from their cotton crop because their labour was cheaper than in the north. Now, though America is a huge market, and produces 22% of the world's cotton, it only exports two fifths of its crop.

Turning cotton into clothes has always been the business of the cleverest entrepreneurs with the cheapest and most mechanically-minded labour. That has not been the case for generations in northern Europe or in the US, where mostly high quality cotton garments are made. Hong Kong (with its post-war influx of cheap refugee labour from China), Korea and Taiwan, with some Portugese and Italian production, now account for most of the cheaper end of the market. In recent years, the US has suffered a huge increase in imports from Third World textile countries, especially China, whose exports to the US rose from 10 million m^2 in 1972 to 500 million m^2 in 1982. Up to a quarter of a million jobs in the US may have been lost to the invasion, mirroring the spectacular decline of the British textile industry. In 1980 US carried a massive trade deficit in textiles of about $7 billion.

Cotton in the US

Rich countries can choose how they grow their cotton. In the US production had fallen by a third between the 1950s and the 1970s, from 3 to 2 million tonnes. In 1925 there had been around 18 million hectares of the crop, which fell to 10 million hectares by 1950, and was down to 3 million hectares by the late 1960s. The proportion of the crop grown for export was rising all the time, as was productivity. Most significantly, the crop was moved westwards, away from the exhausted soils of Tennessee, for instance, and towards soils which were stronger, had been less exploited, and were under the hotter sun which helped the farmer's battle against pests.

Soil degradation in the US remains one of the greatest problems facing the country. As the cotton belt of the 1930s was plunged into poverty by the Dust Bowl, now many western regions of the nation are facing desertification (see **Irrigation** and **Livestock**). The world's largest soil conservation service, that of the US, has not been able to prevent the loss of 12,000 km^2 of degraded land caused by soil loss. This equals the loss of land to non-agricultural development, much of it required by the **automobile**.

The new conditions of mechanisation and better pest control have led the US back into large production which was up to nearly 3 million tonnes by the end of the 1970s. A policy of letting some US cotton fields lie fallow has done its bit to help firm up prices somewhat.

Cotton in poor countries

In many countries, especially in tropical west Africa, cotton is a prime cash crop, but not always profitable. In general, commodity prices, and those for

Resistant species of arthropods and new insecticides 1938-80

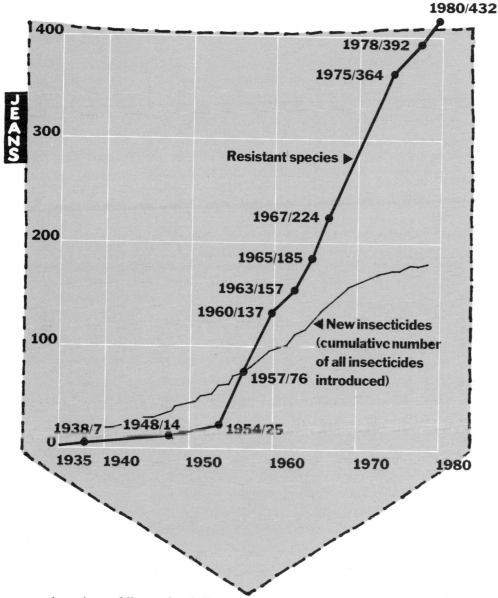

1980/432

1978/392

1975/364

300

Resistant species ▶

1967/224

1965/185

1963/157

1960/137

◀ New insecticides
(cumulative number
of all insecticides
introduced)

1957/76

200

100

0

1938/7 **1948/14** **1954/25**

1935 1940 1950 1960 1970 1980

cotton, have been falling. The dollar price of 1 kg of cotton after adjustment for inflation continues on an abject slither, although it has sometimes peaked, for instance in 1973 and 1976. The terms of trade, however, make this slide far worse. A country growing a cash crop for export mostly thinks of its advantage or otherwise in terms of the imports it buys with its foreign exchange earnings from that crop. The value of cotton in these terms has been moving rather more rapidly downhill: it declined by over a quarter, for example, between 1980 and 1982. A tonne of cotton now buys only a third of the oil it would have purchased a decade ago. (See **Sugar, Coffee**).

In spite of this, the crop, with its high demand of pesticide and fertiliser, remains a favourite. In the Nile Valley, its most famous bastion, it is still grown, even though the farmers there must grow nutrient-demanding food crops when the land should either be lying fallow or be rested with some restorative crop, such as legumes.

In the Sudan the waters of the Blue Nile have been stored behind the Sennar dam to irrigate 800,000 hectares of land in the Gezira scheme, making one huge farm, with a per capita income 6 times that of the rest of the country. Enough cotton is grown by the 2 million people there to create up to 60% of the Sudan's foreign exchange. It is a dangerous dependence, especially since a further 20% of its export earnings are from nuts and vegetable-oil seeds, especially the **peanut**. But up to 70% of Gezirans are infected with schistosomiasis (see **Irrigation**). Malaria is endemic, and diarrhoeal diseases attack children.

In the late 1970s, shortage of capital meant that the cotton crop fell from 1.2 million bales to half that number. The International Monetary Fund, following the latest policy of boosting farm production wherever possible, even at the expense of urban consumers, stepped in with loans and an insistence of drastic reduction in subsidies to urban populations. It probably rescued the fields, but at a cost in unrest which led to riots in Khartoum. Cotton production is now back to normal.

In the 1960s, many poor countries saw cotton as a high-price crop. Mali increased its production by 82% and production in Burkina Faso trebled. In southern Chad, one project tripled both the area and the yield of cotton cultivation. But soil fertility was hardly considered.

Pesticides and cotton

Over 300 million kg of pesticides are used in the Third World every year, around half of the total on cotton. Oxfam, the British aid charity, has undertaken research into the worldwide pesticide industry. They found that in some places, especially the Rio Grande valley of Mexico, almost 300,000 hectares of cotton-growing land had to be abandoned when the tobacco budworm enjoyed a sudden population-growth burst after its natural competitors such as boll weevil were wiped out by pesticides.

The budworm developed resistance to pesticides, in spite of massively increased dosages, which brought in their train increasing health hazards for farmers. Rodents, fungi, bacteria and some weeds are all variously capable of developing resistance to pesticides. It is becoming conventional wisdom that almost any insect will gain resistance to almost any insecticide. Cotton and rice (see **Fish**) are particularly badly hit in the insects' successful war against chemicals.

In some places, up to a dozen insecticides are mixed as a cocktail and sprayed 2 or 3 times a week, and often within 1 or 2 days of harvest. The battle against the diamondback moth on cabbages in the Cameron Highlands in the Malay Peninsular was cited as a case in point by Oxfam.

In the Sudan, yields have fallen by half, and are now at levels similar to pre-

Natural resources used for a bale of cotton

Growing a bale of cotton, 218 kilograms (480 pounds) of fibre, enough to produce 330 pairs of jeans, requires the following:

Production

Input	Quantity per bale
Water	**105,000 gallons/398,000 litres**
Gasoline	**8 gallons/30 litres**
Diesel fuel	**16 gallons/61 litres**
Liquid propane gas	**2 gallons/7.6 litres**
Natural gas	**2,300 cubic feet/64 cubic metres**
Electricity	**60 kilowatt-hours**
Fertilizer: Nitrogen (N)	**31 pounds/14 kilograms**
Phosphate (P_2O_5)	**15 pounds/6.8 kilograms**
Potash (K_2O)	**24 pounds/10.9 kilograms**

pesticide days, when a wide range of competing pests predated the crop, but also each other, rather than the handful of resistant species now found. This is in spite of cotton production costs having quadrupled in a decade, much of the rise being accounted for by chemicals.

In Nicaragua, where cotton production earns around 20% of foreign exchange, in the first few 'chemical years' of the 1950s and 1960s, production boomed. But then, around 1965, disaster struck. In up to 50 applications of pesticide a season, Nicaragua's junkie fields received almost 100 l of liquid and 20 kg of dust insecticides per hectare. Poisoning cases increased, and included around 383 deaths. Malaria here, as elsewhere in the world, strengthened its grip on populations as pesticides applied for other pests became redundant against many species of mosquitoes. Alongside human health problems, crop yields were in decline.

The scale of the human problem is very hard to assess, partly because our epidemiological understanding is slight in these things, but especially so in the Third World where medical records are very thin on the ground. Certainly, the caution which rich countries are now insisting on with their pesticide use is a luxury poor countries have not yet afforded. And it is the case that whilst most of the agricultural beneficiaries of pesticide use, such as they are, are rich – most pesticides are used by labourers on crops and land owned by relatively well-off cash crop farmers – the damage from them is spread a little more evenly. Although the landworker takes a dangerous dose, so too does the consumer, who is usually a good deal better off (see **Fish**). In some cases in the rich world, pesticides intended for non-comestible crops are used on food farms: 10 million Californian watermelons, about a third of the annual crop, had to be destroyed in July 1985 – they had been sprayed with pesticide usually used on cotton.

There has always been anxiety in the rich world that very often it is those pesticides which have been shown to be dangerous, and have sometimes been banned in their home markets, which are sold by Western companies in poor-world countries. Often the marketing of pesticides, especially in the past, has been aggressive: but beyond that, there is the very real difficulty that it requires careful safety measures and precautions – in clothing and practices – to apply pesticides without danger.

In some cases the resistance of pests to pesticides has become so profound that, even granted huge expenditures, pest predations are as big under chemical onslaught as they were when control was hardly practised or was run on traditional lines.

The partly good news

A new hope for pest control depends on a mixture of tradition and modern insights, plus technologies. Called Integrated Pest Management (IPM), it is defined by one leading exponent as 'a broad ecological approach to pest control, utilising a variety of control technologies compatibly'.
This tends to imply

* accepting some crop loss to pests
* treating fields chemically as an emergency rather than routinely
* encouraging insect diversity rather than otherwise, thus allowing natural predations amongst pests
* using biological techniques such as pheromone traps which draw insects to safely enclosed insecticide
* understanding the insect's life cycles much more closely in order to destroy it, perhaps by destroying weeds at the right moment
* rotating crops so as to disrupt the insect's breeding cycles
* growing resistant varieties of crops (especially in cases of mildew, etc)

Much of this is obvious, but not easily learnt in school or in a hurry. Indeed, if it is to solve some of its problems, the IPM actually represents the requirement of the Third World to contrive to be highly educated, but also highly conservative and protective of ancient insights gained over centuries but easily lost by societies (and especially, sadly, by societies which are good at school education).

IPM may be the way forward, but it is far more demanding of skill and time than ever chemical sprays were. It often requires that farmers forgo profit this year and next in order to be able to farm well in three years' time. However logical, that is the sort of carefulness which is more likely to catch on in the rich world than in the poor. As ever, China, in its highly disciplined way, has made a success of the IPM methods. And so has Texas, whose cotton industry had suffered very severely until IPM was introduced.

Picking cotton, Uganda.

19 Irrigation: making deserts bloom, sometimes

GOOD fresh water is almost never where you want it: too little of it in one place, too much of it in another. One third of the earth's surface is either arid or semi-arid and some Indian states are devastated by both drought and flood within weeks of each other.

Though each of us can manage (see **Glass of Water**) providing we drink about 2 l daily, a bit more in hot countries, we need water in large quantities for our crops, which gobble it up prodigiously. A hectare of corn needs anywhere between 6 and 12 million l of water per growing season, and this contributes mightily to agriculture's huge water needs: around 90% of total water use in the USA, for instance.

Some 420,000 km³ of water fall annually on the world's surface, in an endless cycle of evaporation, precipitation and run-off, which depends on the 97% of world's water which is in the oceans. Three quarters of the remainder of our world's water is locked up in the cold polar regions. We harness our rainfall as best we may, sometimes profligately, and sometimes with immense difficulties.

There are around 1.5 billion hectares of worked agricultural land in the world, which makes up about a half of the reckoned potential total. Of this, about 200 million hectares are irrigated, as against 500 million which it is estimated could potentially be irrigated.

In many regions of the world, irrigation can double production; in others, for instance almost anywhere west of the 100th meridian in the USA, it is an absolute requirement for most agricultural crops. Already, the 13% of the world's agricultural land which is irrigated produces 40% of its crops.

Irrigation schemes bring the water which allows an arid region's sunshine to be exploited efficiently, but they add up to only about a seventh of the world's agricultural land. That proportion is far smaller than many agriculturalists would like to see if only the capital expenditure, skills, and higher inputs of fertiliser and pesticide could be found.

Desperate to increase its agricultural yield, India has put $10 billion into irrigation in the past 30 years and wants to spend the same amount in the next 5 years.

China has well over a third of all the world's irrigated land (something like 40 million hectares), whilst China, India, Pakistan, the USSR and Iran between them have over 70% of the world's irrigated land. Israel, using almost all its known water resources, has almost half its 430,000 hectares of cultivable land under irrigation.

Making deserts bloom with irrigation is hugely expensive in water. The 10,000 m^3 of water needed for 1.2 hectares for 3 month crops would supply 100 nomads and their herds for 3 years, or 100 consumers in an industrial city for 2 years. It can also be expensive in energy. In the US well over 3 and perhaps 4 times the energy is needed for a given area of irrigated corn as for corn which relies on rainfall alone.

But granted the expense of energy to run the irrigation schemes directly, which keeps them mostly in the hands of better-off farmers, a further difficulty is that they often form part of a pattern of mechanisation, pesticide- and fertiliser-use which does little for the poor and a good deal for those with access to capital.

Irrigation schemes often promote the disease problems of malaria and bilharzia (see **Dams**). They often also fall prey to the same sorts of difficulties which are thought to have threatened some of the earlier civilisations of the arid areas of the world, especially in the Tigris-Euphrates valley. The evaporation of water from soggy, often hopelessly waterlogged soils leads to the problem of salinisation, since the water's minerals and salt are left behind in increasing, and eventually very damaging, concentrations. Heavy investment, around $650 per hectare in the early 1980s, is required to reclaim such land and return it to productivity.

A tenth of the world's irrigated land is hopelessly waterlogged, and production there has fallen by around a quarter; a similar quantity of irrigated land has its productivity severely inhibited by salinisation. It is a problem which has plagued China, Egypt and Pakistan, where a huge reclamation scheme had to be undertaken on older irrigation works. In the US waterlogging led to expensive reclamation schemes which unfortunately have had the effect of washing salty water down on the poorer farmers of Mexico. Between a quarter and a half of South America's irrigated land suffers from salinisation.

In India there are already great difficulties: about a quarter of the country's 40 million irrigated hectares are in danger of becoming infertile. Indian experience shows that some schemes virtually collapse because there is no incentive to the small farmers to devote labour to their upkeep and development. In one scheme, only a quarter of the area of irrigated land is actually used following widescale dereliction.

In one project in northern India, a tenth of planned irrigation, in what was to be a 300,000 hectare scheme, is actually in use a decade and a half after the scheme's original completion date. Here, the waterlogging problems are such that grain yields have deteriorated, as irrigation schemes turned out to be creating a wet desert. In Pakistan, 100 hectares of irrigated land returns to wasteland every day.

Russia is reckoned to have lost around 7 million hectares of farmland to desertification, much of it to salinisation of irrigated land. None the less, giant schemes to reverse riverflows are envisaged. These schemes will in part be planned to ease precisely the salinisation problem, though they are just as likely to provide new territory for it to encroach on.

Re-inventing the Nile

The Nile waters a narrow strip of Egyptian land, but this 2.5% of the country's land surface supports 98% of its population. American firms are now replacing the 20-year-old Russian turbines of the Aswan Dam, which was President Nasser's great dream-come-true for the Nile's improvement as an agricultural river and power source.

In the case of the Aswan Dam, its associated irrigation schemes have all the difficulties found elsewhere. The absence of flooding below the dam, one of the main purposes for which it was built, has meant that the natural cycle of silt-enrichment has stopped, and now artificial fertiliser, some in the form of nitrates fixed from cheap Aswan energy, are needed to maintain fertility. Rice yields have, however, gone up dramatically, following the increase in perennial irrigation.

In the Delta of the Nile, the world's most fertile region depended for its stability on silt brought by the Nile every year. Now, that cycle has stopped and the future of the Delta lands is uncertain, with the sea encroaching increasingly. The fishery industry of the delta has been disrupted by the absence of nutrients which were found in the Nile's flood water, and the Egyptian 18,000 tonne sardine industry has been lost. On the other hand there is now a 36,000 tonne fishery in the Aswan Dam reservoir, and it is expected to rise.

Bilharzia has spread dramatically, though there is new hope that it can be controlled, and its association with irrigation schemes has more to do with faulty hygiene than with anything inherent in canalising water.

The Aswan Dam was intended to bring new land into production, but by the 1970s, 40% of the new land had gone back to desert. Part of the difficulty was that the new land was worked by huge, bureaucratic farms. Peasants can be rather more efficient in the long run.

Meanwhile, in an attempt to increase the flow of the Nile, Egypt and the Sudan have contracted with French engineers to build the Jonglei canal to divert water from the White Nile from the vast Sudd Swamp, where – it is felt – far too much water is allowed to fester and to evaporate. A digger (whose minders were kidnapped in 1984, in part of the civil war that bedevils the region) which uses more fuel than the regional capital, Juba, to the south, has been slowly gouging out the canal.

Though the Nile's increased flow will probably benefit millions, 1 million tribespeople, mostly herdsmen, of the region will lose their traditional, if

The major water-related diseases of Africa, Asia and Latin America. In the last column, 1 means the sufferer is bedridden; 2: able to function to some extent; 3: able to walk; and 4: minor effects.

Infection	Infections (millions per year)	Deaths (thousands per year)	Average no of days lost per case	Relative disability
Diarrhoeas	**3-5,000**	**5-10,000**	**3-5**	**2**
Malaria	**800**	**1,200**	**3-5**	**2**
Schistosomiasis (bilharzia)	**200**	**500-1,000**	**600-1,000**	**3-4**
Hookworm	**7-900**	**50-60**	**100**	**4**
Onchocerciasis (river blindness)	**30**	**20-50**	**3,000**	**1-2**
Amoebiasis	**400**	**30**	**7-10**	**3**
Ascariasis (roundworm)	**800-1,000**	**20**	**7-10**	**3**
Polio	**80**	**10-20**	**3,000+**	**2**
Typhoid	**1**	**25**	**14-28**	**2**
African trypanosomiasis (sleeping sickness)	**1**	**5**	**150**	**1**
Leprosy	**12**	**Very low**	**500-3,000**	**2-3**
Trichuriasis (whipworm)		**Low**	**7-10**	**3**

extremely frugal, pattern of life. It is hoped that drying out the Sudd will help disease problems, but there is every chance that more new ones will be created or old ones exacerbated.

Wetting the Wild West

The rich world is not immune to the difficulties of water shortage. Of the 30 million km² of the world's land surface which is threatened with severe desertification (see **Livestock**, **Cooking** and **Peanut**), 10.5 million km² are in the US, Canada and Mexico, a good deal more than in either South America or Africa. Overall, the world is losing 200,000 km² of agricultural land a year to desertification.

The Wild West – parts, or in some cases almost the entirety, of the 17 western states of the US – has the clear skies, low humidity and high wind speeds which characterise arid and semi-arid terrain. In spite of the absence of rain, or rather, rainfall of an average of 50 cm or less annually (an almost Middle Eastern climate), the 50.8 million people who live in these states have a per capita water demand of 13,650 l per day, 85% of it for irrigated agriculture. Of this, 5,915 l is 'consumed', meaning that it is not merely used and passed on, but that it is degraded to the point of needing treatment for reuse.

The states of the Great Plains have a huge dependence on agriculture, and thus on water. Nebraska farms 93% of its total land; North and South Dakota and Kansas around 90%; and Oklahoma farms 74%. Even taking account of California, with only 35% of its land in farming, the average across all the 17 states is 67% of land take, as against 38% in the east. They accounted, in 1980, for nearly $60 billion of farm produce, 43% of the US total farm earnings.

Nearly 85% of the land which grows wheat, barley and sorghum (see **Bread** and **Livestock**) in the US is in these 17 states. Of the 'region's' farm earnings, 30% comes from exports. Of the lettuces eaten in New York, 80% are trucked across the continent from California. Oddly enough, the trucking contributes only 6% to the retail price.

Much of this vast production, especially the high-profit produce, is threatened by a simple but severe problem: water is precious in the region. Encouraged by ambitious government subsidies and boundless hope, big water schemes have been undertaken, which especially feed the 20 million hectares that have been irrigated in the western states. Farmers in the west have been allowed to pay far less for their water than either market rates or the cost of getting it to them would have suggested.

One huge and brilliant canalisation and pumping scheme shunts vast quantities of water, around 243,000 hectare-metres a year, from north Californian rivers down to Los Angeles, via the newly rich farmlands of California's Central Valley. But river water is heavily oversubscribed. In the case of the Colorado river 1.8 million hectare-metres of water rights have been granted on a river which produces about 1.7 million hectare-metres in an average year. The use of surface water is going to be fiercely competed for by urban and industrial consumers who can outbid farmers.

The solution adopted so far, of digging wells and pumping up water from immense aquifers, often with little regulation, usually at much faster rates than natural precipitation is replenishing them, leads to a reduction in the available water in the groundwater stores. This process is called 'water mining'. Moreover, there are dangers of subsidence and also of increasing problems of cost in pumping, as oil prices rise and watersheds fall. Groundwater extraction has tripled in the past 30 years, and the percentage of water withdrawals that comes from groundwater supplies has almost doubled.

Arizona is one of the most water-scarce states. It is mining 243,000 hectare-metres from its groundwater supplies, or twice the amount that

"Waterlogging and salinization are sterilising some 1 million to 1.5 million hectares of fertile soil annually."

Worldwatch Institute, Washington, Paper 62, December 1984

precipitation returns to them, and the state government is desperately concerned that the process cannot long continue. Luckily, because it has plans to ease its dependence on farming, there is a good deal of consensus for its plan to rest much of its irrigated land. Arizona plans to let 200,000 hectares of its 526,000 hectares of irrigated farmland lapse by 2020.

The Ogallala aquifer underlies a vast region, and gives up 2.5 million hectare-metres of water a year to them. The 3 states above its southern part (Texas, Oklahoma and New Mexico) have as much irrigated land as the states over the aquifer's northern stretches. However, they only have 12% of its water. Gaines County, Texas, has had to give up most of its irrigation, and a further 400,000 irrigated hectares overlying the aquifer's southern area will probably be out of production within 5 years.

Great Man River Builder

Colonel Gaddafi of Libya wants to become the 'Great Man River Builder', as the nation's postage stamps declared him in 1983. He has initiated a 10 year, $6.3 billion scheme to pump water from deep in the Sahara and pipe it 2400 km to irrigation schemes nearer to his Mediterranean coast. He is hoping to increase the country's growing potential dramatically, and, tired of trying to get farmers to go into the desert to irrigation schemes there, has decided that the water must be brought to the people.

There are some pretty severe difficulties surrounding the scheme, but they are not of the sort, it appears, to worry the colonel. One problem is that it may not work for very long – there is some doubt whether the vast aquifers under the Sahara are being replenished very quickly, if at all, and some of the water is 34,000 years old. The Colonel's scheme may be a classic groundwater mining venture, and the pumping exercise may become prohibitively expensive after a few years. Another problem is that the groundwater of the Sahara may be crucial to the water supplies of Libya's neighbours, Chad, Egypt and Sudan.

The partly good news

Both India and China increased their area of irrigated land by at least 10 million hectares between the mid-1960s and the late 1970s, with the rest of the developing world adding a further 10 million hectares in the same period. Thus, in a little over a decade, the irrigated area increased from 70 million to 100 million hectares in the developing world, whilst the rich world added less than 5 million hectares to its 27 million hectares of irrigated land in the period.

Irrigating maize with bucket and see-saw, in India. This method requires about two hours' work every day.

The potential remains enormous, with perhaps a doubling of area still possible, and an enormous increase in the productivity of land already irrigated. With well-managed irrigation of land doubling, and sometimes quadrupling, its yield, many people see it as providing by far the greatest possibility of increasing production of food in the world. One difficulty is that land that is as productive as irrigation can potentially make it, is extremely hungry for fertilisers. A good deal of research and education is needed to help farmers grow those crops which can nourish the land by nitrogen fixation.

As with many schemes to increase food supplies, such as terracing, irrigation is the kind of project that individual farmers can seldom undertake for themselves. It is an essentially social activity. Thus it may be that the greatest problem with irrigation is that the kind of schemes which can encourage peasants to be productive (smoother markets, lessened financial bureaucracy) may well also diminish the kind of social control or cohesion which previously ensured that the community's infrastructure was kept in good heart.

Beyond that, irrigation- and fertiliser-use require a vast increase in the sophistication of farmers worldwide if they are to be achieved sustainably (see **Jeans**). Almost everything that we know about modern farming suggests that it is a new wisdom, a new ecological and environmental insight, which is needed by farmers. In that, at least, the Third World is not behind the West, where high chemical inputs have in recent years been a substitute for subtlety.

20 A Glass of Water: the simplest requirement

THE most elementary pleasures, like breathing fresh air (see **Cooking** and **Refrigerator**) or drinking a glass of water, in spite of seeming easy and obvious to most Westerners, are very hard tests for civilisation. Our easy complacency that the rich world at least will always provide them is not well founded. Already, there are widespread anxieties about water quality. In the US the very rich are buying 100,000-year-old water, which is presumed to pre-date pollution, trapped as it has been in Greenland's glaciers, at $7 for 1l.

In the Western world, city dwellers are accustomed to using anywhere between 100l and 275l of water a day on domestic uses alone. In the US, the domestic consumption is often over 600l per capita (though this figure varies dramatically between rich and poor), whilst in Britain it averages around 200l.

In the West, about 40% of domestic water is used in lavatory flushing, whilst rather less than that is used for washing people. In many countries, an annual 59,100l of water is used to swill away around 750l of the body's wastes. All around the world, the introduction of piped supplies hugely increases consumption, and often waste.

Gadgets like washing machines have a big effect on consumption: 115l for an average wash is a rough guide. Buying an automatic instead of a twin tub often increases a household's consumption of water by 45l a day alone. Since in most countries all water piped into houses is of drinking standard (potable), increased demand for water for any purpose brings huge problems of sanitation. It is very expensive to ensure that every drop of water that goes into a household is pure.

Growing populations put increasing stress on water supplies. In rich countries, at least there is such massive overconsumption that there is plenty of room for conservation. Los Angeles saved huge amounts of water when it was decided not to sprinkle the verges of some of the roads. During a drought in the late 1970s, people in wealthy Marin County, California, saw their daily per capita domestic water consumption drop from 450l a day to 270l: only their gardening suffered.

A child drinks from a stand-pipe in Nepal: clean water, a basic requirement, may be a great luxury.

Redesign of many gadgets will dramatically reduce water demand. Taking a shower (about 23l of water even in a conventional kind) instead of a bath (around 90l) will help.

Lavatory and cistern design could easily save 40% of the water used in flushing. Simple changes of habit will help: running the water while shaving is liable to take 38l of water, as against the 1l or so which is ample for the purpose. Dish and clothes-washing machines are so often used half or three quarters full that there are considerable savings waiting there.

Along with water savings, there are energy savings in economical use of water appliances. Half of domestic water used demands heating. Halving the use of heated water in the house, not a difficult task, would, it is reckoned, save around 2,250 kWh annually per capita: about 8000 MJ. This is about the same amount of commercial energy (ie, not including gathered firewood and dung) which is available to the average citizen of the Third World, including India and China whose citizens enjoy 4 or 5 times the commercial fuel energy consumption of the very poor (see **Refrigerator**).

How you use water (if you live in the United States)

Direct personal use – 8 per cent of the nation's total, or 160 gallons per person per day, is used for personal and home activities:

Average amount of water required	activity
3 to 5 gallons	**Flushing a toilet**
3 gallons	**Shaving with a blade, leaving the water running**
5 gallons per minute	**Taking a shower**
8 gallons	**Cooking (three meals)**
8 gallons	**Cleaning house**
10 gallons	**Washing the dishes (three meals)**
20 to 30 gallons	**Washing clothes**
30 to 40 gallons	**Taking a bath**

Agricultural use – about 33 per cent of the nation's total, or 600 gallons per person per day, is used in farm and ranch operations:

Average amount of water required	Food produced
40 gallons	**One egg**
80 gallons	**One ear of corn**
150 gallons	**One loaf of bread**
230 gallons	**One gallon of whisky**
375 gallons	**Five pounds of flour**
2,500 gallons	**One pound of beef**

Industrial use – about 59 per cent of the nation's total, or 1,040 gallons per person per day, is consumed in the production of material goods:

Average amount of water required	product
7 to 25 gallons	**One gallon of gasoline**
35 gallons	**One pound of steel**
280 gallons	**One Sunday newspaper**
300 gallons	**One pound of synthetic rubber**
1,000 gallons	**One pound of aluminium**
100,000 gallons	**One new car**

NOTE: About 720 gallons per person per day is used as cooling water for electrical power plants.

Paying for water

In the Western world water has usually been a fairly cheap commodity, and engineers have usually prided themselves on meeting whatever demand there might be. Now, with absolute shortages showing themselves and with increasing environmental costs in developing new supplies (see Kielder, below and **Dams**), one of the fundamental changes which is taking place in the US and UK is the discovery of a market price for water, and a growing insistence that the consumer pay it. Expensive water is far more likely than exhortation alone to make people conserve water.

Damn that dam

In the north-east of Britain, Europe's largest artificial reservoir was made out of a flooded valley of the North Tyne river. Kielder reservoir flooded 1,093 hectares of valley, an 11km stretch of countryside. The scheme cost $196 million when it was finished in 1982, and doubled water supply in the north-east region, in a period – and in spite of water authority forecasts to the contrary – when demand rose by only 1% a year for the decade of the scheme's design and construction.

Whatever the amenity value of a new lake, there remain people whose lives were completely dislocated by the flooding of their homes and land – let alone the expense of the operation and the *folie de grandeur* of the water authority which perpetrated it.

125

Keeping it clean

Only about 10%-20% of the water used in industrial society needs to be of high purity, but a far higher percentage of it is. However, developing separate 'grey' and pure water supplies is too expensive now to consider in most existing built-up areas.

In Britain, about half the water which industry uses is for cooling, and is simply reused later. The people of London, famously, drink water which has been drunk several times by other people before it reaches the metropolis. It passes from the river into treatment works, and back to the river via bladders and further treatment works, only to be extracted again further down. Chlorine, fluoride, ozone treatment and a good deal of time in settling tanks can be required to make potable what may look like pretty clear water.

There are increasing worries about the disposal of human and other wastes (see **Battery**). There are also emerging difficulties about the quality of water we take from rivers (about a third of water supply in the UK), reservoirs (another third) and groundwater supplies (a further third), and which we must make safe enough for drinking.

In the US, which depends on groundwater for about a quarter of its total freshwater supplies, and for a half of whose population groundwater is the sole source of water for their households, there has been widespread anxiety about the pollution of underground water supplies.

Whilst the Third World suffers massive pollution from mostly well-understood sources, in the rich world there is a bewildering range of newly invented substances whose long-term effect at low dosage on humans is unknown. It may take generations for big aquifers and more humble watertables alike to receive the full impact of pollution from the water which seeps down to them bearing agricultural, industrial and domestic wastes. Pockets of potentially dangerous substances can remain immobile in underground water supplies for years, undetected, unsuspected and unpumped.

Problems with nitrate pollution, mostly from agricultural run-off water contaminated with fertilisers, are now becoming far better understood in the rich world. Already there are great anxieties about health risks from this source. American data suggests that every state east of the Mississippi reports major problems with contamination of water supplies, and so do most agricultural states of the sparsely populated west such as Idaho, Arizona and New Mexico. Many of the states which have not reported difficulties are said in newspaper reports to have them none the less. The problems reported include contamination by chemical industry, agricultural, organic, inorganic, domestic and military wastes.

But there remains a central difficulty: the science of understanding long term, low dosage effects of many substances, especially newly made ones, is in its infancy. This is an area in which it is easy for environmentalists to whip up a scare, and easy for scientists to shelter behind mumbo-jumbo: both

"As much as a fourth of the world's reliable water supply could be rendered unsafe for use by the year 2000."

Worldwatch Institute, Washington, Paper 62, December 1984

need a certain modesty in their statements. The environmentalists certainly have it on their side that they are advocating caution. They mostly want to close loops, to insist on waste being reused rather than junked into the environment.

The poor world

A human being needs around 5l of clean water every day for his basic needs. In the poor world, the majority do not get it. Well over half the people in the Third World have no source of safe water to drink. This is in part because 3 out of 4 have no form of sanitation: there is an intimate connection between the two.

The proportion of people living in towns and cities in poor countries who have tap water within fairly easy access has risen to over 70%. This leaves a third, of course, who do not, and the proportion of have-nots will likely rise (see **Birth**). And the tap water is not always safe or reliable. But it is above all the rural poor – probably well over a billion out of the billion and a quarter who are water-deprived – who do not have clean water available to their households.

If about a month's worth of the world's military expenditure (see **War**) were diverted to providing water and sanitation, the World Water and Sanitation Decade, launched in 1980, could have seen its modest annual target of $30 billion met, and the world would have moved towards providing 'clean water and adequate santitation for all' (its slogan) by 1990.

Of course it will not happen, and few countries have dared to suggest even in their most optimistic statements of intention that they are even contemplating such targets. Instead, people drink and wash in dirty water and become prey to waterborne diseases (typhoid, cholera, dysentry, diarrhoea and hepatitis); to water-washed diseases, which thrive when people cannot wash themselves well (trachoma, scabies, yaws, leprosy, conjunctivitis amongst others); water-based diseases, which depend on water-based vectors (especially bilharzia – see **Irrigation**); and water-related parasites (carrying malaria, filariasis, yellow fever, river blindness, hookworm). Perhaps 50,000 people a day die from diseases associated with dirty water.

The people who suffer from one or other of these diseases add up to well over a billion and a half at any time, with symptoms that range from blindness to incapacitation through debilitating diarrhoea (which kills around 6 million children under 5 every year, in spite, sometimes, of expensive treatments which are seldom as effective as clean water would have been). Diarrhoea contributes to the death of 18 million children a year.

The price of water to the world's poor is very high. In some cities, around 10% of a worker's total income might be spent on the water carrier's services. The poor spend a far higher percentage of their income on their very small supplies than even a middle-income, poor-world worker for a much larger, and more likely adequate, supply. In some hilly regions, people may spend over half (and occasionally much more) of their daily personal energy, and around 3-4 hours a day, on fetching water.

21 Dams: the big hope of power and water

ERECTING dams to interrupt the flow of water rushing homeward to the sea is a potent source of infinitely renewable and ecologically safe power (and also irrigation and water storage, see **Glass of Water**). Or is it? Certainly considering the anxieties about acid rain, the greenhouse effect and nuclear waste (see **Refrigerator**), it seems on the face of it a matter for celebration and great future hope that a quarter of the world's electricity (and about 5% of the world's energy consumption) comes from this benign source The potential is something like 15 or 20 times its present exploitation, and much more than that in many poor countries. Already, dam completions planned for this decade will represent a 67% increase in capacity.

Actually, however, both the uses of most of the electricity produced by hydroelectric schemes and the model of development which Third World countries 'buy' when they go for huge dams – usually from foreign banks and foreign engineers – are not capable of helping the poor of this world.

Dams, so far from being appropriate technology, are often highly capitalised, Western-style undertakings which favour elites, not peasants.

Moreover, dam schemes have a habit of running way over budget. The Mahaweli scheme in Sri Lanka saw cost estimates triple between 1977 and 1984. Now the Sri Lankan government must find the equivalent of 3 years' total export earnings to pay for this single venture. The scheme has huge potential benefits: tripling the country's electricity supply, and adding 130,000 hectares of new land under **irrigation** but involving the resettling of 1.5 million people – fully 10% of the population.

The poor of the world need sustainable farming and small-scale industry. Dams in the Third World usually provide energy for large-scale industry, although at immense expense in loan debt which falls on almost everyone in the countries. The Tucurui Dam, one of several planned for the Amazon Basin, is being built at a cash price of $4 billion (see ecological price, below) and will provide electricity for an iron ore and bauxite (see **Aluminium**) smelting industry. But in order to attract this aluminium industry, Brazil is offering firms electricity at one third of the market price.

Thus, aluminium – a metal for export, and, like many cash crops, managed by a world market which militates against the producer countries – will be smelted in Brazil in a way in effect subsidised by the country's poor. Ordinary Brazilians buying electricity from Tucurui will buy it at market prices, but there will be rather few of them since the dam is predicated on created demand by new industries in the north, whilst the domestic electricity demand is hundreds of miles away in the south.

In the Philippines, which is hoping to develop its hydro industry dramatically, Sumatra has developed the Asahan aluminium and hydro scheme, which, at a cash price of $2 billion, will employ only 2,100 of the island's 30 million people. In Iran, the 203m Dez Dam provided **irrigation** water solely to large agricultural enterprises and deprived small farmers of their livelihood.

Big companies have the market clout to do deals which penalise poor countries, especially in a world in which they are themselves heavily pressed by competitors. Kaiser Aluminium did a deal with Ghana for cut-price electricity from the Akosombo Dam on Lake Volta. Completed in 1965, the dam has the fifth biggest reservoir in the world at 148 billion m³. The company tied Ghana to a 30 year contract which today gives Kaiser electricity at a twentieth of the world average price. Any attempt by Ghana to earn more from its bauxite smelting is countered by Kaiser's own need to be competitive and profitable and to keep aluminium competitive with other materials.

Power for the people

"Rural electrification plus soviets"

Lenin's definition of Bolshevism

Lenin called Bolshevism 'rural electrification plus Soviets'. Getting electric light and power to rural communities is a high priority with poor nations. But it has too often been found that only the 'rich' 5%, and those usually in 'rich' villages, can buy the electricity when the power lines go in. In the Third World, 50% of energy development funds have gone to rural electrification for about the last 30 years, yet still only 12% of Third World people live in areas with electricity. Egypt's Aswan Dam, though, with the world's third biggest dammed reservoir, 500km long and holding 164 billion m³ of water, provides 99% of its villages with power.

In many countries where hydroelectricity, especially in small plants, has been ignored for many years, there has been a resurgence in small schemes. France has been notably successful here and now gets 1% of its electric power from modern micro-hydros, whilst other nations – especially Scotland, which was once rich in them – have been neglectful.

In China, 90,000 small hydros have been built since 1968, and these and a few older ones now account for 40% of all hydro power. The government hopes that small hydro schemes will produce 6 times the current energy from small plants.

In India, however, the picture is very different. There are relatively few small schemes and instead a heavy predilection for the large-scale operation. Nehru called dams the 'temples of modern India'; it might be better if the country addressed itself to rather smaller shrines.

The Tungabhadra dam in Central India irrigates 800,000 hectares.

Ecological cost

Dams mean flooding land. Often this is good alluvial farming soil alongside a flooding river. Even when the flooding is part of the scheme's main purpose, for **irrigation,** things may be a good deal more complicated than is at first thought. But usually, the flooding of land is simply an accepted, necessary cost of the dam-building. It is often a rather larger cost than was planned. Beyond the lost production, there are often very large problems associated with rotting vegetation. Many large dam schemes have been bedeviled by acidification of the reservoir water by decomposed plant matter.

In Surinam, a dam scheme at Lake Brokopondo in 1964 flooded 1,500 km^2 of virgin forest whose decomposition led to such severe acidification that the dam's turbine-cooling systems were damaged to the tune of $7 million in a little over a decade.

At another Brazilian dam, Curua Una, which began operating in 1977, similar problems had led to $5 million repair bill for corroded turbines by 1982. In some areas, **fish** have been poisoned by the acidic water at some distance beyond a dam's turbines.

131

In Brazil and elsewhere massive invasions of water hyacinth on artificial lakes also create a huge problem, which costs the environment dear since its clearance often depends on the Vietnam-style defoliant 2,–4D with known dangers to wildlife and people. However, there is some hope that imported manatees – aquatic mammals – may munch their way through the plant in some places.

The rising and falling waterlevels of artificial reservoirs play disastrously into the hands of mosquitoes, bringing malaria, and notably in Brazil, the water snails which bring schistosomiasis (bilharzia). Both these diseases are scourges of many of the natural environments which are sought out as dam sites, and run amock in the new conditions the dam scheme brings. Indian dam schemes are plagued both by mosquitoes and filariasis (elephantiasis).

Part of the problem with dams in many countries is that they are built in areas where soil erosion, often associated with **livestock** or with firewood (see **Cooking**), means that dangerous quantities of silt accrete in dam reservoirs. At the Tehri Dam, which is fed by rivers draining the southern slopes of the central Himalayas, siltation may mean that the reservoir's, and thus the dam's, life will quite possibly be 30-40 years rather than the planned 100 years. In Sri Lanka, peasants displaced by the Mahaweli project have been moved onto fragile hillsides, whose soil is now silting reservoirs.

The Sanman Gorge Dam in China has lost three quarters of its power because of siltation in the Yellow River. Ethiopian peasants and their farming activities 1,600km upstream from the Aswan Dam are creating siltation problems for its reservoir.

In the Philippines, the Ambuklao dam needed 60 years of operation to pay for itself: its reservoir will probably silt up within 32 years and render it inoperable. Some Brazilian dams have already been destroyed by the onrush of water across eroded terrain in the river valleys feeding the reservoir. Several Chinese dams had to be decommissioned before their reservoirs had filled because of unpredicated siltation.

Large dams are often built in very wild places: a dam planned for Tasmania's great wild river, the Franklin, would have irrevocably damaged a world-valued wilderness. In Brazil, many dam projects threaten national parks, including part of Trombetas biological reserve. Sweden and the US have already passed laws which seek to preserve the status of some of their wildest rivers, but these are rich countries where environmentalism is well established.

Dams and people

Large reservoirs almost always involve weighing up the values of the wider community as against those of populations which will be displaced. Aswan displaced 80,000 people; 75,000 were displaced by Lake Volta in Ghana (where resettlement has been bedevilled by problems, not least that the new

Hydropower potential and use, by region

Region	Technically exploitable potential	Exploited resources	Share of potential exploited
	(megawatts)		**(per cent)**
Asia	**610,100**	**53,079**	**9**
South America	**431,900**	**34,049**	**8**
Africa	**358,300**	**17,184**	**5**
North America	**356,400**	**128,872**	**36**
USSR	**250,000**	**30,250**	**12**
Europe	**163,000**	**96,007**	**59**
Oceania	**45,000**	**6,795**	**15**
World	**2,200,000**	**363,000**	**17**

homes provided for peasants came without the patches of land they had always enjoyed for subsistence farming); 57,000 by Lake Kariba in East Africa; and 50,000 by Lake Kainji in Nigeria. An immense dam in China, the Three Gorges Dam, will displace 2 million. In poor countries, these displacements are seldom sensitive or compassionate. The 45,000 people displaced by the Mahaweli project in Sri Lanka were not consulted before the project began, and the compensation most received for being moved 96 km and having to start over amounted to less than $115.

Dams often damage the refuges of some of the most threatened indigenous peoples of the world. In Brazil, the agencies which are supposed to safeguard the lives and lifestyle of Indians have proved wholly inadequate to defend them. In such countries, the tens of thousands of 'primitive' people who are affected by dam schemes are even more tragically involved than the ordinary poor. First, they represent a high proportion of such peoples in the world; second, their sustainable lifestyles are devastated in the name of a progress which would be wholly irrelevant to them were it not for the fact that their lives are destroyed by it.

Some tribal people have already succumbed, within a decade of their first contact with whites, to an alarming cocktail of malaria, influenza and psychological disruption which has led some to suicide by inertia. A few schemes for their sensitive resettlement have been attempted in Brazil, but these new reserves remain threatened by squatters and are not formally or seriously defended by state laws.

The partly good news

The story of big dams and their influence on communities is not wholly bleak. In the case of the vast James Bay Dam scheme in Canada, which is predicated on **aluminium** smelters, and is running into severe financial difficulties, local Cree indians, at first virtually ignored in the planning stages, mounted a vigorous campaign in defence of their interests and have largely succeeded in getting decent compensation. They are said to be coping well with the difficult changes forced on them.

22 Refrigerator: the chilling tale of power consumption

THE average household fridge/freezer (deep-freezers not included) in the Western world consumes about a quarter of the per capita domestic use of electricity. In the energy-extravagant US, this figure drops to about 7%. But that fridge also has an energy-take which is equivalent to about half the commercial (i.e. oil, coal, nuclear, hydroelectric) energy which is available per capita in Africa and Asia for all purposes, including industrial and agricultural, whilst taking only 3.6% (US) or 7% (UK) of total commercial energy available per capita in the West for all purposes. These figures need to be taken with some caution. About 70% of the energy used in the poor world is not commercial but consists of wood or dung (see **Cooking**). About one third of the US electricity generation is for residential use of one sort or another.

At the moment, about 85% of the world's commercial energy is consumed in the rich world. However, the rich world is likely to hold its consumption of energy at far slower rates of increase than is the Third World, since the rich world has the know-how to use conservation techniques, whilst the Third World is at the early, highly energy-hungry stages of industrial development. The poor world's energy-use is also likely to involve older, energy-wasteful, technologies.

It is expected that Third World fossil energy (oil and coal) burning may be 5 times its current levels in about the year 2200, after which pressure on reserves will force a fast decline. Actually, all speculation about the future ought to be treated with extreme caution as we have no idea how diminishing supplies, new technologies, economic growth or market pressures will develop over the next decade, let alone the next century. We can, however, predict that the Third World will dramatically increase its share of the world's fossil-fuel use.

The dangers of burning

Electricity generation normally passes on to us about a third of the energy potential in the fuel used. When we burn fossil fuels we are burning trees.

135

They may be millenia old and underground or under the sea, or they may be modern trees growing on fragile soils, but they remain reserves of carboniferous material which release carbon dioxide when ignited. Since early in the industrial revolution, man has been dramatically adding to the concentration of CO_2 in the atmosphere, which may have doubled as a result of man's fossil and tree burning by the early decades of the twenty-first century.

Because CO_2 in the atmosphere allows sunlight to fall onto the earth, but impedes the return of heat to the atmosphere, a phenomenon known as 'the greenhouse effect' has been identified. This effect is the likely result of modern and future levels of atmospheric CO_2 and is thought likely to contribute to what may be a 2°C raising of the earth's temperature. It is possible that this temperature rise, which will be unevenly distributed, may result in falling rainfall on America's wheat belt, and in Mediterranean regions (including the northern Sahara), whilst the Arab world, parts of Asia and eastern America may experience a rise in rainfall.

Dire predictions of drowned cities (Los Angeles, London, Cairo and New York amongst them) flow from this hypothesis. But it is a hypothesis, and is further confused by our very slight understanding of the world's climate (combined with the theory that we may be overdue for a glacial period, whose interworkings with the CO_2 effect are wholly unpredictable).

The destruction of forests contributes to CO_2 production, by one estimate maybe half that produced by fossil fuels, since they are often burned to clear them (see **Hamburger**). But whilst the oceans of the world are regarded as vast potential consumers of the gas, forest destruction produces a potentially dangerous phenomenon in which the world becomes 'shinier' because of vegetation loss, with further unpredictable effects.

Beyond these effects there is the newly quantified problem of acid rain, which is mostly the result of sulphur dioxide fumes (main culprits: power stations, industry) and nitrogen oxide fumes (main culprits: **automobiles**, power stations and industry) released into the air. The chemicals make rain and mists acidic, and seem to have a remarkable power to wreck the leaves of trees. Their effects on vegetation – including a capacity to release other toxic chemicals already in the environment – are beginning to be clear.

Acid rain damaged the vast peatlands of Britain's highlands as early as the nineteenth century. Many lakes in northern Europe suffer from acidity, which kills fish life. Acid rain may prove more damaging than we can now recognise, especially as its corrosive effects on buildings may last long after any policy moves are taken to reduce acidity. Besides, its effects are not yet understood. It is said, for instance, to be reacting with the atmosphere, under sunlight, to produce damaging ozone.

Culprits are scattered all over the industrial world. East Germany and Czechoslovakia are especially bad offenders, the latter because it burns high-sulphur coal. Czechoslovakia produces almost 3 times as much sulphur dioxide per citizen as Britain does.

"Speak now or forever hold your breath."

Protest banner hung from a US utility smokestack

Nitrogen Oxide emissions in selected countries

	United States	Canada	W. Germany
Quantity of Emissions *(million metric tons/year)*	**19.3**	**1.83**	**3.0**
Sources of Emissions *(per cent)*			
Transport	44	61	45
Electric Utilities	29	13	31
Industries	22	20	19
Homes, Businesses	4	5	5
Smelters, Misc.	1	1	—
Total	100	100	100

Sulphur Dioxide emissions in selected countries

	United States	Canada	W. Germany
Quantity of Emissions *(million metric tons/year)*	**24.1**	**4.77**	**3.54**
Sources of Emissions *(per cent)*			
Electric Utilities	66	16	56
Industries	22	32	28
Smelters	6	45	—
Homes, Businesses	3	4	13
Transportation	3	3	3
Total	100	100	100

Techniques do exist for reducing the emissions which cause acid rain. They are expensive to introduce, and the US and Britain are world leaders in arguing that they might not halt the threat to lakes and forests. The electricity

137

generating industry appears to have played ducks and drakes with admittedly very complex evidence. Ironically, however, many of the available techniques for reducing the sulphur content from our smokestacks will increase the consumption of coal per unit of electricity, and that might worsen the greenhouse effect.

Thinking about energy

Whether the greenhouse effect or acid rain will turn out to be as dire as is predicted by some experts is anyone's guess. Certainly, many governments round the world – notably, perhaps, the US and UK, and most in the Third World – are not inclined to jeopardise their hopes for growth, which are in any case unlikely to be fulfilled, by allowing conservation-minded scientists to influence policy too much.

Simple economy may lead to the conservation of energy, rather than ecological imponderables. Unfortunately, even with increased conservation in the West, per capita levels of consumption there are still likely to seem impossible dreams, incapable of fulfilment to the citizens of the poor world. Should any global policies of conservation of fossil fuel seem necessary, either to preserve supplies or diminish ecological effects, it will be impossible to win worldwide acceptance for them unless there is far greater equity in international consumption levels.

The world community will not act unless everyone's interests are seen to be roughly of a piece. We are a long way from that yet. Both CO_2 production and the creation of acid rain are believed to be capable of cure at source, though still only expensively, and while this may be acceptable to rich consumers, the question still arises of whether the Third World would be prepared to fall into line.

Nuclear

Oddly enough, anxieties about the ecological effects of fossil-fuel burning may lead us into an increasing interest in the nuclear process (see **Uranium**). The nuclear industry takes some delight in noting that conservation measures such as draught-stopping and better insulation in houses have led to far greater doses of radiation for most people than ever the nuclear industry has. Radon gas, a danger to **uranium** miners which has also become relatively more concentrated in modern energy-saving houses, accounts for around a third of radiation dosages for most people, as against 0.1% from nuclear industry discharges. Medical uses of radioactive material account for over 10% of an average person's radiation dose, whilst 87% is natural.

By some counts, the burning of coal for electricity in the US produces 10 times the loss of life expectation (roughly speaking, the days or weeks an average life is diminished) than would the same amount of electricity generated by nuclear power. But this takes no account of the anxieties about a cataclysmic accident in a nuclear station, the nuclear bomb connection, or the huge imponderable of nuclear waste disposal.

No one wants nuclear waste near their town, and there is increasing anxiety that dumping it at sea is hardly responsible. Some poor countries, China amongst them, have been looking at becoming waste-handlers to the world. In 1984 Japan had to shelve plans to sea-dump some of its waste when non-nuclear Australia and New Zealand protested at the scheme.

The nuclear debate is not well conducted. Too often the nuclear industry and its governmental sponsors have been caught out in their over-confidence about promoting the technology. They have usually used bizarre accountancy to make investment in nuclear power seen rational, when in reality it was merely a virility symbol for politicians, and held out the promise of loosening dependence on coal miners and Arab sheikhs, neither of whom are entirely predictable as groups. Meanwhile, as epidemiology becomes more sophisticated, the mapping of cancer occurence does seem to point to incidences which can be traced to possible routine nuclear discharges, and less routine ones (see **War**). Meanwhile, evidence mounts that UK nuclear safety officials have allowed as normal doses of radiation which may be 15 times higher than is wise.

The anti-lobby, sometimes equally over-enthusiastic about their case, and operating on a shoe-string budget, will certainly, if nothing else, go down in history as having exerted a discipline on the industry which it seemed ill prepared to exert for itself.

Energy conservation

Some of the most important energy conservation measures are in our own hands. Already, US domestic appliances are about 50% more efficient than their 1975 counterparts. Danish designers are working on the assumption that fridges could readily be constructed which would have less than a quarter of normal consumption of electricity. Modern Japanese fridges, costing little more than US types, can save 1,000 kWh of consumption a year (out of a normal US standard of about 1,400 kWh). A bike will go for 566km on food energy the equivalent of 1l of fossil fuel. An extra sweater and turning the lights out when one leaves a room go a long way to cutting house electricity bills.

Energy conservation work of the most basic kind in British buildings would create jobs and save nearly $6 million a year in energy. Using ordinarily available techniques, most domestic heating costs in Britain could be cut by at least a half and perhaps three quarters. If US **automobiles** could average 10km per litre (itself around double the petrol consumption that is easily attainable), the average American would save 15,910l of gas across the 10-year life of the average car, which itself could easily be doubled and thus create more jobs (see **Jobs**).

A \$200 voice-sensitive switch saved one British school 30% of its fuel bill. Heating metals directly by electrical resistance (current run through them) can make big savings in industry. Lasers have been found to cut fuel consumption by 90% in some energy-expensive industrial processes. It is not surprising, perhaps, but it is a very hopeful sign, that Japan, hard hit by the oil-shock of the 1970s, is rediscovering the technology of the waterwheel, which, with modern developments, can produce electricity at half the cost of ordinary utilities.

In one exquisite development, a northern Californian utility found that it was cheaper and more profitable to encourage and subsidise its customers to insulate their homes and save electricity than it was to build the power stations which might have satisfied profligate and increased demand. The utility took a lot of persuading of this counter-intuitive insight. It was the US Environmental Defense Fund which pointed out this peculiar route to profit. An account of this is given in *Dynamos and Virgins*, by David Roe, Random House, New York, 1984.

Global CO_2 production.
This 'business-as-usual' energy scenario assumes zero energy growth in the USA between now and 2025, 2% growth in Europe, 4% in the USSR and Eastern Europe, 4.5% in China and 1.5% in the Third World. On this basis, making likely assumptions about the fossil fuel use of each region, CO_2 emissions by 2025 will be six times those of 1974. But the Third World and China, which are likely to rely heavily on coal, will be putting out a far higher proportion of the world's CO_2 in 2025 than they are today.
(Note: US etc includes Canada; W. Europe etc includes Japan, Australia, New Zealand; USSR etc includes East Europe; China etc includes N. Korea and Vietnam.)

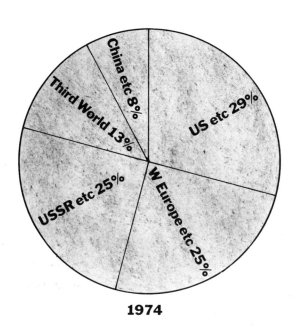

1974

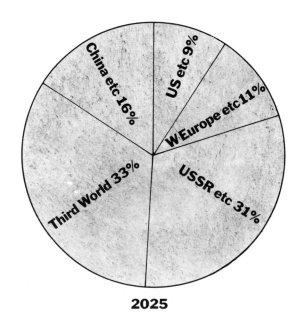

2025

23 Cooking: wood, the growing fuel

IN the rich world, wood is used for cooking as a matter of nostalgia by people who are less impressed with its properties as an extremely polluting form of heat, than by its romantic evocations. It is simply vital, however, in many Third World countries which lack both piped or wired sources of energy and the money to pay for them. Countries such as Chad, Benin, Tanzania and Burundi use wood for well over 80% of their total energy supply.

'For more than a third of the global population, wood is the primary source of energy, and for another billion people, wood fulfills more than half of their fuel needs,' says the United Nations Agency for International Development.

Yet firewood is in severe shortage in many places. In parts of Africa, Asia, the Caribbean and Latin America, average consumption of wood runs at a tonne a year per person. It is often gathered as dead wood as near to centres of habitation as possible, rather than plundered from living forests and scrubland, and many Third World cities are surrounded by a zone in which firewood gathering has long been impossible. Approximately 100 million people around the world have been characterised as being in acute shortage for fuelwood needs, and about a billion and a half are dependent on sources which are being depleted dangerously, rather than 'farmed' for sustainability. By one estimate, the world will need 2.6 billion m³ of fuelwood a year by 2000, but only 1.5 billion m³ is likely to be available. In some cities, people pay a third of their income to obtain fuelwood, whilst in other places women may spend a whole day simply gathering the wood required for 3 days' cooking.

With painful slowness, governments and aid agencies around the world are trying to work out how to encourage people to grow trees – an unconventional crop which has the added disadvantage of being relatively slow to grow. In some cultures, community-based ventures work well, whilst in others, people are finding that giving land to poor people to farm trees commercially is more appropriate.

Gathering fuelwood is not a major source of destruction of virgin forest in

> **"... I trust you will agree with me that no forest legislation and no forest policing action will succeed in keeping the hungry away from the forests."**
>
> **Edouard Saouma, UN official, 1984**

the world. We lose 14 hectares of tropical forest every minute, but relatively little of it is lost to firewood. Nor is the international trade in wood (much of it for housing and lorry-building) the major consumer of tropical forest wood. According to some analysts, perhaps 5% of the wood taken from the world's tropical forests goes into international trade; the rest is used or wasted in the producing countries. The tragedy is that much of the timber simply goes up in flames, or is left derelict in forests as a result of careless logging practices. Forest clearing (see **Hamburgers**) can be very crude, and commercial logging often destroys many more trees than it troubles to extract from the forest resource.

The international forest trade cannot be entirely blamed for one of the main effects of its operation, though it is part and parcel of the destruction of forests which often begins with pioneer work loggers do in opening up forest terrain. Roads are blasted through the forest and the clearing work begins making it possible for squatters to move in and convert the forest to rough pasture and arable land. Nor is logging inherently disastrous. Recent research has shown that forests can be harvested on a commercial scale far greater than their traditional uses by hunter-gatherers, and can become profitable as well as sustainable resources. But that will take care, expertise and political will. Indeed, since the world tropical forest resource is concentrated in relatively poor countries (some of them, such as Brazil, with huge debt problems), it is likely that where national interest does not dictate conservation of natural habitat, only international funding can.

Timber, USA

The USA, though the world's largest timber producer (mostly owing to geography), has only half the quantity of forestlands of the USSR. The USA is also the world's largest importer of timber, and runs a deficit in its timber balance of trade. Its imports are mostly from Canada, and never more so than with a strong US dollar in recent years. The US plans to become a far greater producer of timber than it is at present, and to become self-sufficient in its timber needs.

...and Brazil and Chile...

The 60% of Brazil's land surface which has forest cover, about 500 million hectares, contains about a third of the world's remaining hardwoods (those most prized for furniture and other high-value uses). Brazil is reckoned to have reserves of about 16 billion m³ of forest wood, but exports only around half a million tonnes of sawn timber a year. At present rates of destruction,

8% of its vast forest resource will have been lost by the year 2000. Its forests are far less valuable hectare for hectare in timber terms than those of the Far East. In Chile, one million hectares have been afforested for commercial use, and there are hopes that Latin America may obtain around half of its timber – instead of the current 1% – from plantations. Of the total Amazon rainforest, about 3.5 has been damaged. This all sounds mild enough, but the inequity of the land ownership – which drives the landless into the rainforest – and the haphazard way the forest is exploited rather than harvested create widespread anxiety that the plunder will lead to irreversible destruction.

...Asia...

Many Asian countries are using their forests as one-off cash resources. In many countries, forests cannot long survive this maltreatment. It is reckoned that Thailand's forests may be destroyed within 15 years, Malaysia's in 25, and the Philippines' and Indonesia's in 40-50 years. Thailand is losing 10% of its forests (which account for around 20% of its groundcover) every year. The market is selective, but the forest destruction is not. Less than 700 out of the 3,000 main species of trees in Malaysia have commerical value, and of those, only 400 are marketed. Indonesia (whose main customers include Japan, taking almost three quarters of the country's total exports) plans to expand the value of its timber exports by around 20% a year. Some of this increase is being achieved by processing the wood at home. The peninsular Malaysia (selling about half its wood within Asia, about one third to Europe and 1% to the US) is losing 200,000 of its 6.2 million forest hectares every year.

To provide firewood and to reduce soil erosion (25 million Indians a year suffer from flooding), India needs 3 times as much forest cover as it has. However, instead of instituting much-needed reafforestation programmes, the country eliminates about a million hectares of forest a year, and replants less than half a million.

...and Africa

Much of the African tropical forest is being destroyed with precious little regard to its real, sustainable possibilities of providing wood. The Ivory Coast, a major hardwood supplier, may become a net importer: its 15 million hectares of dense forest has shrunk to 3 million, and is continuing to do so at about 400,000 hectares a year. The country mostly exports its wood as sawn timber, which is worth very much less than processed wood; its major customers including Italy, France, Portugal and Spain, where it is used mostly for plywood.

"Ouagadougou in Burkina Faso has its own 500-hectare green belt; and ... when the public is involved and knows it will share in the eventual harvest from the trees, it protects the forested areas from overgrazing and fuelwood poaching, an onerous task that could never be adequately achieved by professional foresters."

Robin Clarke, in *Ecology 2000* (Michael Joseph, London, 1984)

Collecting wood – a daily task for many African children.

Some customers

Japan is by far the biggest importer of forest products in the world. Usually a great protectionist, Japan allowed other Asian countries to suffer deforestation whilst husbanding her own resources. For years she did well out of importing sawn trees, which she processed at home into usable timber; now most countries want to keep the processing for themselves.

The Japanese import almost $5,500 million worth of forest products (excluding paper and pulp) annually; the USA and the UK over $2,000 million worth each (but these two import a good deal from their neighbours as well as from the tropics). In the UK it has long been regarded as scandalous that the country has ignored forestry whilst instead heavily subsidising farmers to produce wheat and milk, both of which are in chronic surplus.

Wood and this book

Every day, 450 million people buy a daily paper, doing their bit towards the annual world demand for 29 million tonnes of newsprint (the paper newspapers are printed on). A further 42 million tonnes of other sorts of paper are produced every year, many of them used in the 0.75 million book titles produced annually. Broadly speaking, a sheet of paper consumes twice its weight in wood. It takes over 3,000 tonnes of paper to produce 1 issue of the Sunday *New York Times*.

The average citizen in the rich world uses about 18 kg of newsprint a year (as against 1.5 in the poor world), and about 30 kg of other printed paper (as against 2 kg in the poor world), whilst around a further 200 kg will be consumed by the US citizen in packaging.

Paper for rich-world consumption is mostly made from conifers grown in countries such as Sweden, Finland and Canada, where the crop is managed very strictly by government controls. Sweden, dependent for 20% of its export earnings on the forest trade, has headed off a potential shortage of wood supply by changes in husbandry in recent years.

The paper industry can be extremely polluting. In the USA and the USSR there have been major scandals about the effluent discharged from paper plants into rivers and lakes.

24 Uranium: the basis of latter-day alchemy

Nuclear power, as we know it now, begins with uranium and its radioactive properties, though, if we ever truly imitate the sun, and use fusion power, we will be released from this dependency. We dig uranium from the ground and, in our power stations, we turn it into some of the nastiest stuff known to man. The used uranium fuel rods contain highly radioactive waste products of fission, as well as reusable uranium and plutonium (which sceptics say is more prized for its bomb-making properties than for its avowedly peaceful uses, in nuclear power). The wastes of nuclear power produced now will not be 'safe' until the end of the twenty-sixth century, and no foolproof containment for them has been discovered.

However, if the problems of disposing of the finished product are desperately imponderable, we can at least say that we know a great deal about the real costs of producing the uranium in the first place.

Ironically, much of the world's usable uranium, needed for a process especially valuable to the rich world and replete with environmental dangers, occurs on lands which belong, or ought to belong, to some of the world's poorest people. In some of the territories where it occurs and is mined, it threatens the way of life of people whose traditions are rich in notions and habits which respect the fragility of the earth.

Uranium mining takes place in the US, South Africa, Canada, France, Niger, Australia, Gabon and the USSR. The poor countries with uranium supplies have been especially badly hit by the wild price fluctuations in the world market. Niger, in particular, was heavily dependent on its royalties.

The world recession has dramatically reduced the increase of the rich world's use of electricity, and made conservation seem more attractive than consumption. Uranium prices have tumbled, from around $66 a kg in 1980 to $37 in mid-1984. This has forced producers to use only the cheapest sources of uranium, unless, as in some countries, the utilities have long-term contracts to pay on a cost-plus basis.

Careless mining of uranium and disposal of the 'tailings' (mining wastes) exposes workers and neighbouring populations not only to the normal hazards of mining, but also to dangerous levels of radiation. In recent years, mining operations in rich countries have been dramatically improved, but even so there is a legacy of cancer amongst miners from previous, less regulated days. There are also problems in Canada and America's New Mexico with radioactive pollution from tailings contaminating underground water resources.

The South African uranium industry, supplying most of Britain's uranium, is shrouded in a good deal of state and corporate secrecy, but it is known that the black South African and Namibian mine workers have worked in radiated environments that more open societies have banished.

In the US

It was a Navajo herdsman who is reputed to have led uranium prospectors to the first American uranium ores. It is a moot point whether his doing so conferred any great benefit to the indigenous peoples of America's southwest. In the 30 years since that incident, New Mexico has become America's crucible of uranium mining, and nearly half the country's uranium is mined in the region, not far from the Los Alamos Scientific Laboratory, which first researched the atomic bomb.

Indian tribes own one half of the privately owned uranium in the US, and rank fifth in the world as uranium owners, until recently producing on their trust lands around 10% of the world's uranium. The Navajo, Spokane and Laguna Pueblo peoples accounted for nearly a quarter of all US production in the early 1980s. This contribution by their national land – granted to them in the sure expectation that it was worthless – to the national economy has still left the average Indian with an income one sixth of the white average, and a jobless rate 10 times that which obtains nationally.

Those who are employed in the industry do get large salaries, but even on the 'richest' of the uranium reservations, unemployment hovers at 25%, and per capita incomes are a good deal lower than elsewhere in the US. They have not been helped by the sporadic rises and falls in the price of uranium to which their royalties, often around 15%, are pegged. In the wake of the difficulties experienced in the nuclear power industry, and of world over-production of uranium, they have found that their reward for the environmental and social disruption they endure has shrunk.

The health risks associated with uranium mining are hard to assess, partly because early indifference to them meant that there was no pre-mining testing of radiation levels, and partly because the epidemiological science of assessing the incidence of cancers is, even today, still in its infancy.

Certainly, the mines on the Laguna land, notably the Jackpile Mine, the world's biggest (it closed in 1982 as a result of falling uranium prices, adding further unemployment to the Laguna's problems), have been run on worryingly makeshift lines. Many tribal leaders were anxious about safety standards, though these being surface mines, there is supposed to be very

> "The Great Chief sends word he will reserve us a place so that we can live comfortably to us. He will be our father and we will be his children. So we will consider your offer to buy our land. But it will not be easy, for this land is sacred to us ... If we sell you land, you just remember that it is sacred, and you must teach your children that it is sacred and that each ghostly reflection in the clear water of the lakes tells of events and memories in the life of my people."
>
> Chief Seathl, in a letter to President Franklin Pierce, quoted in *Vole Magazine* April 1980

147

much less radiation risk to workers. It is in deep uranium mines that sophisticated ventilation techniques are required to make working safer.

It took a visit in 1978, by Robert O. Anderson, powerful chairman of Atlantic Richfield, which had recently taken over ownership of the mine, to reassure tribal leaders that their message of concern was getting through to the people who held the purse strings. In the wake of the visit, many improvements were made, accompanied by warnings that increased costs would threaten the economic viability of the operations, and might hasten their closure. However, when the closure came, Atlantic Richfield gave aid to the tribe in the hope of helping them weather the uranium recession.

There is hot controversy now about disposal of the millions of tons of tailings which have arisen in the south-west, Utah and Pennsylvania, as a result of uranium mining and milling (the process of extracting useable metal from ore).The degree of threat this waste poses to water resources is not properly known, and appears to have been the occasion of a good deal of fudging by the US government, in spite of anxieties expressed by the official Environmental Protection Agency. Environmentalists and local officials fear that recent regulations have loosened controls and safety standards unacceptably.

In spite of the present uranium recesssion, many states in the US, Wisconsin and New York amongst them, have seen moves by mining corporations to stake claims on uranium sources, bringing the threat of environmental despoliation nearer to the articulate and affluent American citizen, and ensuring the prospect of further over-production and its attendant seesaw price cycles.

Australia

With no nuclear power stations of its own, Australia's anti-nuclear sentiments have been expressed in powerful opposition (itself powerfully countered) to uranium exploitation in the country. The bulk of Australia's uranium is found in the north of the Northern Territory. Over 70% of the country's reserves are in the traditional stronghold of Aboriginal culture, and development of them has long been seen as a major threat to the Aboriginals.

The difficulty is compounded by the strong pattern of ownership by overseas mining interests of Australia's mineral resources. In 1980, 40% of Australia's uranium mining projects were foreign-owned, and successive governments have pressed to increase Australia's stake in its own mining future.

With Australia's 10% stake in world uranium production, the country has a powerful and anxious interest in the current massive surplus of the mineral. In 1983 there was a world 180,000 tonne stockpile, sufficient for 4.5 years' supply. Australia's government, in allowing present projects to proceed, is likely to be helping the lowering of world uranium prices in its attempt to maintain an income from uranium. Australia has the largest reserves of low-cost uranium in the free world.

Cheap energy at any price

There never was cheap energy. From slash-and-burning in the Stone Age, (and now – see **Cooking**), through coal and oil burning, all of them of course using carboniferous fuels, to nuclear power, with its promise of releasing man from ordinary combustion, there have been huge costs to be paid for our demand for heat.

Nuclear power, famously, brings with it a new kind of threat, that of uncontrollable genetic changes in the world's species which may echo throughout the future as a result of mankind's incurable optimism that we can solve the problems associated with our latest discoveries. This is not to say that nuclear power is not capable of becoming a decent technology: but certainly we do not yet know how to make it so. Even if we did, the civil programme is so interwoven with the military demand for nuclear material that we cannot really talk of nuclear power as being a civil programme. Uranium has a terrible capacity to end up in destructive use. This has not happened before. Previous fuel revolutions merely produced quicker ways of getting TNT to the enemy: uranium's uses include new devastation.

25 Gold: luxury and danger

"I should be pleased if it turned out that the entire soil is a colossal mineral deposit which, once it is mined, will leave the whole area one gaping hole." Adolf Luderitz, German trader, 1884, of Namibia's mining prospects.

Quoted in *A Future for Namibia 3: Mines and Independence* (Catholic Institute for International Relations, London, 1983)

Man has always been in love with gold. Its rarity (its average distribution through the earth's crust is 0.0035 g per tonne) and great beauty have ensured it an enduring place as a medium of exchange and, in alloy form to overcome its extreme weakness, ornamentation. All the gold ever mined would make a cube of only 18 m on each side.

The jewellery trade takes around two thirds of annual production, though this varies widely from 1,000 tonnes to less than a quarter of that. Gold used to be vital in electronics, which accounted for around 7% of gold use in the late 1970s. But new technologies have reduced its importance. None the less, firms in the West have started to beat up old computers, mining from them the 1 kg of gold per tonne of printed circuit found in machines which have become obsolete. Dentistry takes about 7% of world supplies.

In bullion form, but no longer as coinage, gold is still the bedrock by which currencies are backed around the world, though its role has declined. The US government holds around 8,000 tonnes. Nowadays, the holdings by governments are most important in the effects they have on the value of hoardings by individuals.

The French have a tremendous yen for gold. A large share of individual wealth – a figure of $20 billions worth was suggested in the late 1970s – is held in gold (around 4,615 tonnes in 1981). The West Germans are great hoarders, taking around a tenth of the annual gold production, and around a third of the 3 million Krugerrands produced every year. Each Krugerrand has just 28g of fine gold.

In India, with a strong Hindu predilection for gold, the 5,000 tonnes of the metal in private hands is vital to the pawnbroking and banking system. Russians like gold too. In the course of a year, of all the people in a particular mine whose jobs meant they could get their hands anywhere near it, 5% were arrested for smuggling.

Gold is very widely distributed in the world, and there have, throughout history, been gold rushes in countries as diverse as Egypt, Russia and the US. There is now one in Brazil, and production increased by a half between 1982 and 1983. Ghana, with 30% of export earnings coming from its export of around 11,000 kg of gold, intends to double production before 1990.

World production is running at around 1,100 tonnes a year, which implies that the world's exploitable reserves of 35,000 tonnes may well come under pressure over the next couple of decades. Already, old mines are being reopened, and in Australia new techniques have been developed to exploit what had been regarded as unprofitable reserves.

South Africa is now by far the leading producer, with 657.6 of the 1,231 tonnes of 1981 world production, and around 680 tonnes in 1983. Other countries trail far behind: the USSR with 200 tonnes in 1981, perhaps 260 in 1983, Canada with 49.5 tonnes in 1981, the US with 40.6 tonnes in 1981, other African countries combined with 40 tonnes in 1981, Brazil with 35 tonnes in 1981 and Papua New Guinea, Australia and the Philippines all with around 25 tonnes each in 1981.

South Africa's gold production is, of course, extremely controversial. Governments, liking it or not, must do business with the country for their **uranium**, diamonds and gold, the last of which contributes upwards of 40%, nearly $12 billion, of the country's vital export earnings, and well over 10% of the country's tax revenues.

South Africa has, in the past couple of years, been hit simultaneously by falling gold prices, partly due to rising supply and slack demand, and a severe drought. The country is now experiencing its worst depression since the 1930s. Its per capita income has been falling swiftly. Nearly a quarter of its blacks are likely to be unemployed over the next few years. The red tape of racism – running the country's apartheid policies – is itself a huge burden, with a third of whites employed by the government, many of them in the administration of racism.

For South Africa, there is nothing like world inflation to cheer the government up, since it normally increases the value of gold. In recent years falling inflation rates in rich countries have helped reduce gold prices, and have drastically affected the country.

South Africa goes to great lengths to exploit the 500 km arc of gold reserves which make up the Witwatersrand system, stretching from Evander to Virginia. The difficulty is that they are persuing an elusive seam of gold which is seldom more than 2 m thick and runs at depths of up to 5000m.

Exploration costs have risen tenfold in recent years, but new finds increase only slowly. To develop one new mine is reckoned to have cost $230 million: it will employ around 750 whites and maybe 10 times as many blacks.

South Africa's mine safety

South Africa has had an appalling record of mine safety. Partly this is because many gold mines are deep, often up to 3,700m, and often worked by inexperienced miners, amongst whom, as might be expected, there is a very high turnover rate.

In 1982, accidents amongst the half million workers in South Africa caused almost 600 deaths, and over 15,000 workers were badly enough hurt to be off work for over 2 weeks. In that year there was a payment of $55 million in pensions and compensation to accident victims. In the Transvaal and Orange Free State the death rates for white miners was 0.70 per 1,000, but 1.65 for blacks.

The fatality rate nationally is about 8 times the death rate of British miners. The past decade has seen improvement in some mines, but the accident rate remains high, in spite of many improvements in techniques, because increasingly more dangerous mines are being worked, or reworked, in pursuit of the increasingly rare metal.

South African mine-workers

A decade ago, only 1 in 4 of the black workers in South African gold mines was South African, but recently, Malawian, Mozambican and Zimbabwean workers have been sent home. Now it is mostly South African blacks who work the mines, earning upwards of a seventh of the average white wage, as against the twentieth which was their share a decade ago. Real wages for black gold miners had been static for half a century until the early 1970s.

Now, unionisation is growing in the 100-year-old gold mining industry, after a recruitment drive beginning in 1982 by the fledgling National Union of Mineworkers, which claims around 150,000 members in a third of the 43 South African gold mines. The union was set up by the Council of Unions in South Africa, one of two main black workers' organisations. It has made great strides, including the acceptance that strike action be made legal. In the summer of 1984, 12 miners were killed and 1000 injured in strike action. In August 1985, the NUM struck against three hard-line mining companies and was foiled. It was a bitter defeat for the leadership, who had been successful in negotiating with Anglo-American, a firm with whom it had developed better relations. The 14-20% pay increase won by black miners for July 1985 left them still far behind their white colleagues.

Black workers live in single-sex hostels, whether they are migrant in the normal sense of having come from foreign countries, or 'migrant' in the South African sense, namely coming from the 'homelands' which South Africa has created within its borders. 'Migrants' from South Africa's 'homelands' now make up around 97% of the 420,000 black workers in the industry. The National Union of Mineworkers has been allowed recently to recruit amongst foreign black workers as well as amongst 'migrants'. Its attempts to increase the chances of blacks getting responsible work in the mines (for instance, by being allowed to train for blasting certificates) have been bitterly opposed by the reactionary white Mine Workers Union, which is determined to keep a strong colour bar in the mines.

Tribal rows, rows over pay and the meat ration at meal times, and

Opposite: scrubbing freshly poured gold bars, South Africa.

disagreements with their home governments (foreign workers in South African mines are often paid their wages by their government of origin) have contributed to the toll of violence in recent years.

Principal uses of gold in the USA

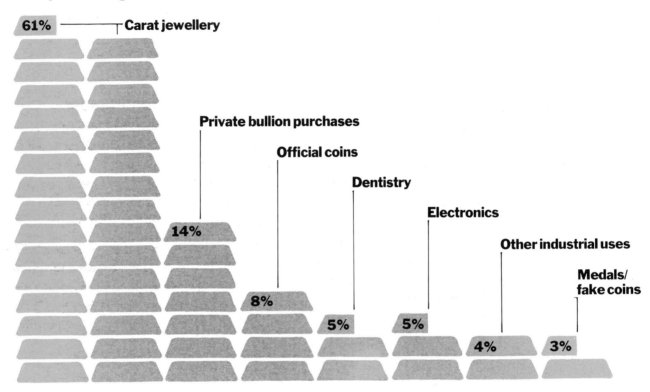

61% ──────┬ **Carat jewellery**

Private bullion purchases

Official coins

Dentistry

Electronics

Other industrial uses

Medals/ fake coins

14%

8%

5%

5%

4%

3%

26 Aluminium: the commonest modern metal

ALUMINIUM is a particularly twentieth-century metal: its uses, its production, its sources, are all newly discovered. The hard, light, durable and conductive nature of the metal was early seen as a great advantage; its sole difficulty was that it required 20 times more energy to extract from ore and process than did iron. Aluminium is the most abundant metal on earth, but 80 million tonnes of bauxite, the 'mother' ore of aluminium (named after Baux, the French Mediterranean village where it was first, but is no longer, dug), must be mined to produce the 14 million tonnes of aluminium currently produced every year.

Aluminium was and is mostly mined in poor countries for use in rich ones. Bauxite is especially common in the tropics and sub-tropics. It had the advantage to its rich users that its ore and the energy needed to refine it are often found together in poor countries. This matters because energy costs contribute about a third of the overall aluminium production budget: it requires around 18,000 kWh of electricity to produce 1 tonne of aluminium from 2 tonnes of alumina.

To produce aluminium, the mined bauxite ore is crushed and dehydrated. These mining operations have caused environmental degradation in countries as diverse as Australia and Jamaica. The bauxite is then washed in hot caustic soda solution to extract alumina. The aluminium and the oxygen are then separated out of the alumina by electrolysis. It was the discovery, in 1886, of the new electrolytic process that allowed bauxite to be turned into aluminium with far greater ease than previously, even though it required prodigious quantities of coal. It turned a precious metal, which had so far only been used in the jewellery business, into a light metal for industrial and domestic use.

The low cost of aluminium now made it available for ordinary uses, for example, being highly heat conductive, for cooking utensils, rather as iron smelted in England's Severn Gorge first found a mass market as cooking pots. The metal was then used for far more exotic purposes in the burgeoning electrical, aeronautical and automobile industries. The use of natural gas, and then of hydroelectric power, followed, as the few firms in the business widened their quest for cheap energy.

"If steel was the workhorse of the industrial revolution, the light metal has become the queen of the newer technology bridging the gap from railroads to rocket ships."

Industry commentator, 1937, quoted by Ronald Graham in *The Aluminium Industry and the Third World* (Zed Press, London, 1982)

Before the turn of the century, the price of the metal had fallen from \$32 a kg to less than \$1. Consumption of the metal rose tenfold in the years 1890-5.

Production roughly doubled every decade throughout the first 7 decades of this century. The story is of large companies (and still only a handful have 70% of aluminium production) which governments have tried periodically to control, but which have always been able to rely on government support.

Aluminium goes to war

Two world wars massively increased rich nations' dependence on secure supplies of this, the ultimate warfare material. Aluminium had, by the end of the First World War, become the crucial munitions metal, with wood and iron inappropriate to the developing airplane industry. Fierce competition for, especially, Jamaican bauxite supplies strained relations between the US and Britain. Ships, trains and bridges were using aluminium, and its uses had so diversified by the mid-1930s that **automobiles**, which previously had taken 60% of aluminium production, were by then taking a relatively humble 14%.

Three quarters of a modern airplane is made up of aluminium and its alloys. The metal is replacing copper as the main component of electrical wire. In 1915, aluminium output was one seventh that of copper; now aluminium production by weight is double that of copper.

War has always been a big consumer of aluminium: the US smelting capacity expanded sevenfold during the Second World War, and the companies – often the target of government trust-busting attempts – received vast loans and cheap electricity to aid their expansion.

Aluminium economics

In spite of a picture of great exploitation and much manipulation by powerful companies in poor countries, actually aluminium production has never been an easy capitalist business. Huge investments and low rates of return make it financially hazardous. Consumer governments attempt to control prices through their own vast military requirements. However, their attempts have usually been thwarted by their periodic sudden needs which put them back into the hands of suppliers, usually of their own nationality, who are themselves then squeezed by their vast energy requirements.

More recently, world overcapacity and a world slump has forced aluminium production to decline, with severe effects in almost all producing countries. In Britain, a Scottish plant had to close, not least because the cheap nuclear power on which it was predicated never materialised.

None the less, the poor countries with the bauxite, and later with the cheap energy supplies, have always been the ultimate and most serious losers, since the small gains they make can never compensate for their poor competitive position vis-à-vis the firms and each other. It is very galling for them to own the resources rich countries need, but never to benefit much from doing so.

Jamaica, under the Michael Manley government in the mid-1970s, managed to impose new ownership patterns and higher taxes on the mostly American firms mining its bauxite. The country saw its aluminium income rise nearly tenfold as a result, but has since been the victim of retaliation: by US firms, who moved what production they could elsewhere; and by other producing countries who have been undercutting them. All this took place in the wake of the OPEC oil price hike, and the foreign exchange earned by bauxite sales was even more badly needed than before. Indeed, there are OPEC-imitation attempts at producer-cartels in bauxite countries, in much the manner that there were attempts to organise **banana** producers.

In the wake of the world recession, Jamaica's position has worsened. In 1982 its bauxite output dropped by almost a third.

The aluminium dilemma

Historically, by the 1960s, the position was clear: poor countries produced the ore, and were sometimes in the position of undertaking the separation of the alumina from the ore, but the final smelting was confined to rich countries. Now, in the 1970s, those countries with cheap hydro power, rich and poor alike, are increasingly operating as smelters, not usually of metal they own and not often profitably. This is even true in the case of the Volta River region, Ghana, which both mines and smelts, but none the less must import bauxite. Describing the distortions created in poor countries by this pattern, Ronald Graham, in his The Aluminium Industry and the Third World, (Zed Press, London and Lawrence Hill, Westport, Connecticut, 1982) says,

> Infrastructure – roads, ports, railways, hydro-schemes, etc., – was designed by the foreign corporations for their own profit maximisation. Resources were unevenly developed with only certain parts of the production process being located in the resource-rich countries.

The countries have had little choice but to accept the chance to earn royalties on their production and to be glad of any development of infrastructure that has come their way (even if it is useless to most of their citizens). The alternative would have been to do without either, and see the small advantages go elsewhere. This is the true cash-crop dilemma, only this time the harvest is inorganic and finite.

The search for power

Though the power demand for each kilogram of aluminium had plummeted from 40 kWh to 15-25 kWh, the search for cheap power became crucial during the 1950s. For many years Iceland, Norway and Canada provided the bulk of the cheap hydro power which the burgeoning industry needed. But after the Second World War, firms began to look to the Third World for their power just as they already did for their bauxite, with the Gold Coast, Malaya, Borneo, Sarawak, Indonesia, Guinea, British Guiana and Australia amongst the potential sources.

It was perhaps not surprising that many hydro schemes (see **Dams**) in Uganda, Central Africa, Ghana, Indonesia, Papua New Guinea and the Philippines did not prove the great boon to their countries that was expected when they were first 'sold' to those countries. They had been designed to produce cheap power to foreign companies, rather than geared to spark off an autonomous industrial development. Especially following the oil price hike of the 1970s, many countries intensified their search for hydro. Japan in particular had to relocate its smelting industry, and went abroad to Indonesia, Australia and Papua New Guinea instead.

Aluminium is the *raison d'être* of many hydro schemes. Even in the highly developed Pacific north-west of the US, the metal consumes a third of the hydro power produced. In Canada, which in early 1984 for the first time allowed aluminium beverage cans, Alcan Aluminium have started to exploit the new market. They have the advantage of paying around $48 per tonne of aluminium for the electricity used for the smelting as against the average of around $284. The company is charged around 17% of world prices for its electricity.

The future of aluminium

For many of its constructional purposes, aluminium is now being threatened by the prospect of energy-cheap plastics which are increasingly combining strength with their well-known lightness. Car manufacturers are looking to plastics to replace aluminium, itself the wonder material of a decade ago.

There has for many years been chronic over-production of the metal. Around 1 million tonnes of aluminium are stockpiled around the world. These stocks will have to be mopped up before any increased demand, predicted to come in the next few years, will be turned into price rises for producers.

Recycling aluminium

Though much energy is required in making aluminium from alumina, the metal itself is recycleable very cheaply. It is thought that 80% of aluminium in use could be recycled at the end of its 'first' life. In mature economies a large amount of aluminium is available, for instance in domestic durables; in late starting economies, much of the aluminium consumed is in goods which are still in their prime and will thus not enter the recycling stream for several years.

Energy-starved Japan now uses more recycled scrap than primary sources in its aluminium production, some of it at least as bits of Toyotas and Datsuns in their second crossing of the Pacific Ocean.

Recycling is important because it requires 20 times more energy to make aluminium from bauxite than it does to 'produce' new aluminium from scrap. At the moment, about a third of aluminium production worldwide comes from recycled scrap, but around half of that came from smelter and production scrap rather than from the reuse of aluminium goods. None the less, aluminium recycling is one of the bright spots of environmental policy and has increased dramatically in recent years.

One quarter of US aluminium production goes into packaging, and half of that into beverage containers (see **Carbonated Drinks**). The 2.5 kg of aluminium that the average US citizen annually consumes for beverage containers alone matches the total aluminium use of the average Mexican. Partly on grounds of litter, but also to save energy, the US beverage industry has accepted, and at times even instigated, recycling ventures. Many states, ranging from the first, Oregon, to the latest, New York, have legislated for a deposit system on beverage containers, to encourage recycling. Where there is legislation insisting on deposits for containers, around 90% of beverage containers are reused, in the case of bottles, or recycled, in the case of bottles and aluminium cans (though not tin-coated steel cans which are notoriously difficult for recyclers).

These initiatives contribute dramatically to the 54% recycling rate for total US aluminium cans, and, perhaps best of all, it has been found – in spite of early anxieties on the part of unions – that such moves create jobs. However, they do demand a shift away from primary production and towards the secondary recycling industries. The US General Accounting Office believes that a new nationwide – rather than the present patchy – beverage container deposit law would create a net total of 100,000 jobs.

27 Automobiles: private versus public mobility

"Tell me how fast you go and I'll tell you who you are."

Ivan Illich
Energy and Equity
(Marion Boyars, London, 1974)

THERE are something like 350 million cars on the roads of the world. We have achieved this astonishing figure from scratch inside this century, and in particular since 1959, when there were a mere 50 million cars worldwide, of which two thirds were in America. Even now, the US has almost twice as many cars per 1,000 population (516 per 1,000) as western Europe (244) and both 'outcar' India (2) monumentally. The US's share of world car possession remains at 41%

The paved road came with a bang to the US: from non-existence 100 years ago, to 3 million miles now, on which run 9 million new cars a year. There are almost 2 million new cars registered annually in the UK and 1,000 in Malawi. An average American can expect to travel around 15,000 km annually by car, a European will do around 6,500 km and in the Third World the figure would likely be zero. If the average American car was merely as efficient as the average car in the rest of the world, the saving in fuel would be roughly twice the total fuel consumption of the fifth of the world's population that lives in China.

The car consumes 10% of US gross national product; 15 million Americans, 22% of the workforce, depend on the car industry for a living. Americans spend around 15% of their personal income on automotive transport. Of all the gasoline consumed in America, one third goes into cars, and in western Europe around a sixth.

The prime costs of the automobile age are: the death of public transport, pollution, congestion, consumption of valuable oil, land used for highway construction, and the distortion of an individual's perception of his mobility.

The death of public transport

A country can have a public transport system which delivers equitable transport (including hire cars and taxis, which have been subsidised in awkward rich-world districts and at awkward times at about a hundredth of the cost of subsidy needed to bus the routes). Or it can have the private car and a debilitated public transport system which will increasingly be the third-rate, inadequate prerogative of the poor, young, old and infirm with the very rich travelling in splendid isolation in first class on some routes.

There is no certainty that a country can have both, unless the public subsidy of transport is to be phenomenally large. However the World Bank stresses that public need not mean publicly-owned. Throughout the Third World there are city bus firms which make profits where the state or municipality's service on the same routes can not.

In the US during the Second World War, when public transport was at its height, 19 billion passengers annually rode the nation's streetcars and subways. City public transport use had fallen by two thirds by the early 1970s. In America, 85% of intercity travel of over 160 km is by car, and this on journeys usually beautifully suited to public transport.

Los Angeles has 3.3 million motorised commuters morning and evening, and 77% of the cars have only one person in them. It is estimated that 320 million car km a day are made in southern California. Trains and buses now have 3% of the intercity market, which is ideal for them.

In Europe, two thirds of intercity travel is by car. In Britain in 1952 the private car had one third of the total mileage travelled, but by 1968 it had claimed three quarters of a vastly increased total (mileage had doubled). In the meantime, public transport's share had shrunk from two thirds to less than a quarter. Britain, at least, is not a country which needs the mass dependence on the private car: 30% of all journeys are of less than 2 km; half of all journeys are less than 8 km long; and half the journeys to work are made by car, in spite of often being ideal for public transport or the bike.

Much of the advantage enjoyed by cars derives from spending by the state which would have been better directed at public transport systems. US governments have traditionaly spent at least 5 times as much on roadmaking as on subsidy to public transport (though, admittedly, some of the road-making benefits the bus, which remains, however, less potentially efficient than the train).

The US Interstate Highway System has cost the tax payer $225 billion for its 68,380 km. A further $50 billion is needed to complete it. It now costs $16 million to build 1 km of Interstate Highway, and between $31 million and $63 million if it's in a city. This compares badly with $13 million for 1 km of railroad. In the past decade the American taxpayer has spent $80 billion on highways and $6 billion on railways.

In Britain, many cars are bought by companies as perks for their employees. As such, they enjoy a substantial tax advantage which would not accrue if the firms gave the employee more cash in the paycheque. Thus, the tax community is paying for the private individual to run a car which helps debilitate public transport. The cost to the British exchequer is put at $460 million a year. That is a straight subsidy to private as against public transport; a subsidy to the individual to pit himself against the community.

A well-loaded city bus or train can take a passenger 53 km for 1 l of fuel. In

> "Between 1950 and 1973, cycle traffic was reduced to less than half its earlier level in most European cities ... but ... in recent years sales of cycles have exceeded those of cars in most countries."
>
> *Running on Empty* by Brown, Flavin and Norman (W. W. Norton, NY, 1978)

the country, buses give well over 70 passenger km to 1 l, and trains close to 140. But because we do not use our public transport systems well, a more likely city average is 14 passenger km per litre, taking the busy rush hours and the deserted off-peak hours together.

Amtrak, the heavily subsidised and suffering American railroad, may average 14 passenger km to the litre, whilst Greyhound buses on intercity routes get closer to 41. None the less, even on Amtrak, a decently loaded line in the north-east will deliver 28 passenger km per litre. A – very rare – fully loaded little car with – very rare – good fuel efficiency will deliver 35 passenger km to the litre in town, and 63 out of town. Averaged out, the British country bus is 1.5 times as fuel efficient as the car.

Los Angeles freeway: cars cost.

Public transport struggles on bravely: though UK bus passengers have declined by two thirds since the mid-1950s, the total distance travelled by buses has fallen only by one third.

The advantages of trains and buses over cars are immense. By any proper cost computation, a rural bus fare is about a half of the equivalent cost of running a car the same distance.

Cars congest streets

A train can accommodate 1,400 passengers, who would require a 1.6 km-long convoy of buses, or 636 cars strung out over 32 km of road. Meanwhile, the congestion caused by cars in cities costs a lot of money. If the Monday to Friday services they run could go at the same sort of pace they manage on easy Saturdays, London Regional Transport say their buses would be 15% quicker, and surveys indicate that another 50 million people would use the services. This would provide a further $14 million in revenue, on top of the $35 million saved every year. In a typical medium-sized city, 1.6 km per hour improvement in speed would release 40 buses for new routes or higher frequency on existing routes.

Cars immobilise people

Of all British households, 40% have no car. Therefore, around 16 million people are without direct or family access to a car. Only 30% of women drive, while only 70% of men have licences to drive. No one expects that car ownership in Britain will now extend beyond about two thirds of households. Even for those households with a car, the majority of members are deprived of mobility once the breadwinner has driven off to work.

The car and land

The car consumes land at an alarming, direct, rate: 6.5 hectares per km is the motorway average in Britain. But adding in junctions and service stations, the figure is brought up to nearer 10 hectares. In central London, the car accounts for only 11% of journeys to work, but it takes 85% of the road space. A 3.7m-wide road devoted to bikes has 5 times the people-carrying capacity as one twice as wide devoted to cars. One fifth of a modern city area is now devoted to the car.

But the car also takes land indirectly. Because of the 'LA factor', in which modern people are assumed to be car-mobile, industry, schools, shops and hospitals are sited at greater distances from one another. The land-take per person in the West is therefore growing rapidly, in urban sprawl. The hearts

163

of cities die as the car chokes them and renders them increasingly unattractive, whilst people flee to the suburbs and beyond in their commuter cars.

The car and safety

Every year in Britain cars kill or seriously injure over 50,000 people (about half the population of Cambridge, or the entire population of Apache County, Arizona). In America, about that number are killed outright in car crashes every year.

One of the costs of the car has been the threat it poses to the bicycle. As many bikes are sold in America and Britain as cars (annually, about 10 million each in the US, about 1 million in UK) but cycle distance does not increase in proportion to sales. In Britain, about a fifth of bikes are never ridden, and one survey revealed that the dangers of competing with other vehicles on the road was the largest issue in people's minds in their not using bikes.

Drunken drivers kill around 25,000 annually in America, and injure around 650,000. American youngsters (under 24 year olds) make up only 20% of the country's drivers but are involved in more than 40% of fatal accidents involving drinking. When Connecticut withdrew its High School driving school subsidy, it was found that fewer teenagers were getting licences, and fewer still were involved in car crashes.

Seat-belt wearing in America, it is reckoned, would save 10,000 lives annually, and $2400 million of the immense health and wage loss bill incurred because of the car's propensity to crash. Such legislation in the UK, for the compulsory wearing of front seat belts, is reckoned to have cut the number of hospital casualties from car accidents by a fifth, saving perhaps 700 lives and 7,000 serious injuries.

What it takes to make a car

Over a third of the energy-take of the automobile comes from its production and maintenance, and about 60% from the fuel used to run it. The biggest contribution to car fuel efficiency now seems to be achievable through weight reduction (an American car averages about 1700 kg, and a European car about 1200). An increase in the percentages of **aluminuim** and plastic and new alloys of steel are reckoned to be the profitable routes, though difficulties may arise if the complicated new metals or plastics cannot be recycled easily. A high percentage of the vehicles currently scrapped every year (1 million in the UK alone) are recycled.

The saving in fuel in propelling a lighter car is reckeoned to be nearly 35 times the extra energy cost in producing the **aluminium** (as opposed to steel) from which it would increasingly be made. A car produced with proper attention to corrosion will likely to have a potential life of up to 20 years, double our current expectations for most cars.

We can however mourn the 2 tonne, gas-guzzling, distinctively chunky, checkered cabs. Such a feature of American life, they are made no more at a factory in Kalamazoo, Michigan after a 25-year spell. Long-legged people, and children who like riding on jump seats, will now have to use the back seats of ordinary saloon taxis – or come to London.

Cars and pollution

Motor vehicles (including lorries) in Britain add around 8 million tonnes of carbon monoxide, 1.5 million tonnes of unburnt hydrocarbons, 500,000 tonnes of nitrogen oxides (see **Fridge**), 140,000 tonnes of particulate matter and 1,200 tonnes of lead to the environment each year.

The main present attack on motor car pollution has taken the form of improving exhaust systems, with 'catalyst converters', to soak up some of these gases. Unfortunately, it costs $500 per car, is easily cheated, and only works when the engine and exhaust are running hot. A new generation of engines is being designed which burn very 'lean' fuel and are far less dirty. Some car firms, whilst arguing for this new technology, have had to accept that some European governments appear to be drifting toward the 'catalyst converter' solution. Meanwhile, speed controls – especially in high-speed countries such as Germany – look likely to be able to reduce pollution and road deaths simultaneously and immediately.

In Germany, a good deal of acid rain pollution (see **Cooking**) has been blamed on the exhaust of cars and its relationship to high ozone levels. Similarly, in the western states of the USA, scientists believe that car pollution is largely to blame for acidification there. Clearly, fewer, smaller, cleaner cars are needed if people and forests are to breathe easy.

Cars and private lives

A lovely insight into the nature of industrial society came from Ivan Illich, in his *Energy and Equity* (1974). It is worth quoting direct:

> The typical American male devotes more than 1,600 hours a year to his car. He sits in it while it goes and while it stands idling. He parks it and searches for it. He earns the money to put down on it and to meet the monthly instalments. He works to pay for petrol, tolls, insurance, taxes and tickets. He spends four of his sixteen waking hours on the road or gathering resources for it. And this figure does not take account of the time consumed by other activities dictated by transport: time spent in hospitals, traffic courts and garages; time spent watching automobile commercials or attending consumer education meetings to improve the

quality of the next buy. The model American puts in 1,600 hours to get 7,500 miles: less than five miles an hour.

In countries deprived of a transport industry, people manage to do the same, walking wherever they want to go, and they allocate only 3% to 8% of their society's time budget to traffic, instead of 28%. What distinguishes the traffic in rich countries from the traffic in poor countries is not more mileage per hour of lifetime for the majority, but more hours of compulsory consumption of high doses of energy, packaged and unequally distributed by the transport industry.

28 Computers: the new world – horror or lazy paradise?

ALVIN Toffler, author of *Future Shock*, has characterised this present and the immediate future age as The Third Wave, and wrote a book to prove it. First, man became agricultural; next he became industrial; and now he is the possessor of the microchip. Liberated from heavily centralised political and economic structures, the modern and future individual can live a richer personal, domestic and social life in which we are all informed about, and inform, the world without Big Brother, the state or any other similar impositions on our autonomy. If we are lucky.

It is anyone's guess whether Mr Toffler will be right. There are those who agonise that computers, information technology and robots will tyrannise us before we manage efficiently to enslave them as the most powerful helpmates ever devised.

The revolution has been dramatic. In 1946 the world's first electronic computer was at work in Pennsylvania. It occupied a large room, had 18,000 vacuum tubes and used the same amount of energy that a steam locomotive needed. Nowadays, a computing machine of the same power costs $100 and runs on torch batteries.

From valves to integrated circuits, via the discovery of transistors, the development of the computer has moved apace, and will go much further still. During the past decade, the number of components that could be fitted on a silicon chip has doubled every year. The result has been that the cost of a given amount of computer memory has been slashed to a fiftieth during the 1970s, and a typical component's cost fell to a hundredth. In the last 5 years of the 1970s, the number of components fitted to the average chip rose 100 times, and the number is expected to rise one hundredfold over the next decade.

An industry that did not exist at the end of the Second World War is now worth hundreds of billions of dollars a year, ranks in the top handful (after steel, cars, chemicals and farming) and produces machines which range from the trivial to the profound. *Computerworld* magazine has suggested, 'If the auto industry had done what the computer industry has done in the last 30 years, a Rolls-Royce would cost $2.50 and get 2,000,000 miles to the gallon.'

'The technology is inescapable, what we create is a matter of choice."

Joe Engelberger, 1984

One electronic telex machine has a single microprocessor in place of nearly 1,000 moving parts; its manufacture cuts labour requirements to a third of that required by the mechanical type. The first 5 years of the 1970s saw NCR, an American cash register firm, switch to electronic machines, with a labour 'saving' of 75% and a halving of its US labour force. The company saved rather more in its European workforces: one plant in Dundee, Scotland, shed four fifths of its labour force. The Swiss watch industry, based on high quality clockwork, lost 46,000 jobs as the world switched to digital watches. Digital watches are now so cheap that in the US, a quarter of the population buys at least 1 watch a year.

Electronics in the print industries have typically cut jobs by a quarter and increased worker output by 50%. Some newspapers have cut their compositing staffs by more than half as a result of computer technology. The new generation of televisions, with more micro-electronics replacing cumbersome circuitry, and automated production, has enabled manufacturers to cut their labour forces by up to a third, whilst increasing output from individual plants by a quarter. Already in the textiles industry, plants are opening which employ less than a quarter of the people in traditional factories.

Electronics in the office have extraordinary implications for firms. The editing and printing of office documents can be made anywhere between 50% and 100% cheaper. It costs 45 times more to store information on paper than electronically. One major implication is that by equipping a manager with a work station (word processor, data terminal, etc) which costs less than a secretary's annual salary and about a third of his own annual salary, a manager can be freed from the need to employ clerical assistance. Electronics take the drudgery out of documentation and information handling. A high proportion of the secretarial and clerical workforce is therefore under threat.

Information technology does not merely have implications for the rich world. Microprocessors are cheap and have already found application in the mechanical sorting of **coffee** and rice crops in such a way that diseased or inadequate beans or grains can be discarded with extraordinary speed and ease. This method goes some way towards eliminating the dangerously high wastage which besets poor farmers.

In the heat of the turmoil of such a revolution, it is difficult to gainsay those who insist that though jobs are lost, they will be taken up elsewhere. However, the new technologies do not so much create new things to do, consume and make (as did the old transport and manufacturing booms of the nineteenth and early twentieth centuries), as change the way we make many goods and perform many services we already have or do. They make many tasks labour-free.

However, by making products less dependent upon labour, the new technologies may give rich countries an advantage in making products which are currently labour intensive – a further difficulty for the Third World.

Whilst 15 million American homes have video games connected to their televisions, and there is now an $8 billion per year video-game industry in the US alone, few people have yet found that the sharp edge of the computer revolution gives them the kind of change in consumption that, say, the Victorians could have claimed for the train, or modern people for the car. Their televisions and washing machines do much the same jobs as they did before the micro era, though perhaps a little quicker or in a smaller cabinet. The changes are taking place far more dramatically in their working lives, and in ways we have barely comprehended yet.

Robots: metal, muscle and mind

The computer threatens secretarial and clerical jobs; the robot threatens 'oily rag' jobs. Accurate, strong and tireless machines will threaten the blue-collar world in the same way that computers will revolutionise the white-collar world. However, domestic robots face many difficulties: an automated vacuum cleaner, for instance, must be able to recognise the house kitten in order not to consume it. It is reckoned that it will take several years to develop machines clever and cheap enough for this market.

There are only a few tens of thousands of industrial robots in the world at present. Japan leads with perhaps 30,000 of the more sophisticated, industrial, reprogrammable robots, around 65% of the world total, and 50,000 simpler, single task devices. Japan has around 200 robot-making firms,

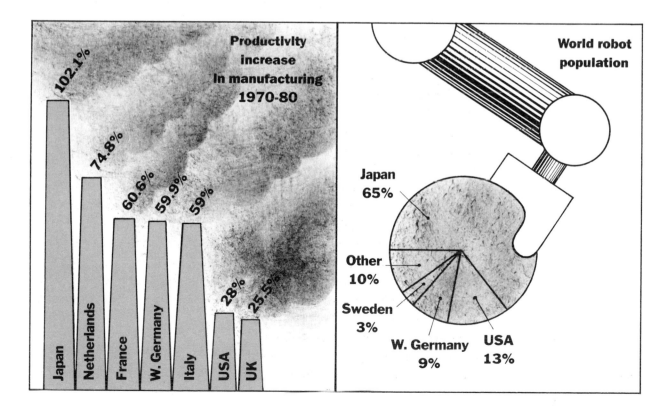

Productivity increase in manufacturing 1970-80

102.1% Japan
74.8% Netherlands
60.6% France
59.9% W. Germany
59% Italy
28% USA
25.5% UK

World robot population

Japan 65%
Other 10%
Sweden 3%
W. Germany 9%
USA 13%

producing 17,000 machines a year. That country uses almost all its own robot production, making its yearly uptake of robots approximate to the total number of these machines outside the country: there are perhaps 1,500 in the UK and 6 or 7 times that amount in the US. They have phenomenal power. In the car industry, American plants have often found that production can rise by 20% and labour forces be reduced by 10% with robotisation. Some British car plants believe that robotisation can double car production per worker. British Leyland's Austin Rover group has seen production per man rise 130% since 1979, of which 40% is put down to new technology.

Fiat's Strada body shop produces 1,200 car bodies a day, employing only 25 people – and robots. Robots offer the prospect of routine tasks perfectly and tirelessly performed. But they also offer the potential of far greater flexibility than human assembly workers, since they can be programmed to new or altered tasks by computer. Westinghouse Electric Corporation, which now owns Unimation, is working on the 'clever' robot and the US is hopeful of establishing parity with Japan in the production of future generations of productive machines. A British company has developed a 'seeing' robot which can weld continuous seams, one of the least pleasant jobs in a car factory. But the use of robots is being restricted by the difficulty of integrating them with orthodox factories: they outperform their neighbours on production lines, creating bottle necks. A futher revolution in robotics looks to follow the pattern of computers with a move towards cheap, off-the-shelf machines which will flexibly perform lightweight tasks.

Environment and computers

The new-age technology is supposed to be clean and nice, compared with the dirty old 'smokestack industries' which belch unpleasantness into the air. The truth is less comfortable. Silicon Valley, a 200 km² area south of San Francisco, is plagued with pollution difficulties affecting its groundwater (see **Glass of Water**). Solvents, gases and acid used in etching and cleaning silicon chips, the nuts and bolts of the revolution, have been seeping into the area's water sources. Of 98 Silicon Valley storage sites which have been inspected 75 have leaks, and there are fears (not yet scientifically proven) that birth defects may have been caused as a result.

The Fairchild Camera and Instrument Corporation of San Jose ran into difficulties when an underground tank was discovered to be leaking. A local well which supplied 16,500 households was contaminated with 1,1,1,-trichloroethane, a degreasing solvent that can damage the central nervous system, liver and heart. 14 million clean-up dollars later, the firm was further subjected to lawsuits claiming damages.

In the wake of the disclosures, IBM, Hewlett Packard, Tandem Computers and National Semiconductor are all believed to have found leakages from their storage tanks, of chemicals which cause disorders in the respiratory and nervous systems.

Further difficulties have arisen from the new 'clean' industries' smokestacks. California's smog in part includes emissions from high-tech firms. The emissions from evaporating solvents are highly polluting. However the authorities have insisted upon new measures, including carbon filtering and the incineration of wastes, which will help to cut down the emissions by the required 3.5 tonnes a day, but will cost the industry an estimated $10-14 million.

There are several major difficulties with any assessment of modern toxic pollution: one is that we are at the outer limit of our understanding when we try to assess the immediate and long term problems associated with breathing or drinking low levels of complicated new chemical entities, yet we are often faced with the illegal dumping of difficult chemicals into the public waste disposal system. Public waste management systems at present operate a holding operation in which many wastes are never actually dealt with but merely stored in a more or less dispersed and diluted form.

Though chimney scrubbers have been installed at the request of the authorities, many of them are said not to work well, and it is especially hard to regulate activities of small firms.

Almost 1.5% of US electronics workers are said to suffer from industrially related diseases, as against less than 0.5% for the average of American workers. Acid burns, eye problems and skin irritations are ranked high amongst the electronics related problems. Headaches, dizziness, burning tongues, nausea and flu-like symptoms are also claimed to be common. Some workers have claimed that it was the electronics industry which caused their 'chemical sensitisation' (also known as 'environmental illness').

Commuting or computing

According to one study, based on the employees of a large insurance firm in Los Angeles, the average employee travelled over 32km per day (kmpd) to and from work. The average for urban workers is a little under 32 kmpd. The higher the individual ranked, the greater the likely daily distance travelled, until the top executives were notching up well over 48 kmpd. The firm's workers' totalled 19.9 million km, which burned up 37.4 million kW a year.

The Third Wave has the potential to check this travelling. To move people costs more than to move information. A phone line uses 1 watt whilst it is in operation, and the average computer terminal manages on 100 or 125 watts. The study reckoned that work done at home with a computer as against work done at an office combined with commuting has an energy advantage of nearly 30:1 if the commuter uses a car to get to work, and over 10:1 if the commuter uses public transport. Taking 1975 figures, if less than 15% of urban commuting had been replaced by computing, the US could have saved its entire petroleum imports bill.

In the late 1970s, Ivan Illich, the philosopher who refuses to appear on television, argued in a letter to me that he was better employed travelling in an aeroplane (of which he disapproves) than in recording a video tape and sending that instead. Doubtless, we all much enjoyed his conversation when he visited; but the point is worth making that it is, in general, far less polluting and energy profligate to send an image or message rather than a person across large distances.

Women and electronics

There are few sources of information about the human costs in the Third World which arise from electronics, most of whose extremely labour-intensive manufacture takes place well away from unionised and pricey Silicon Valley or other Western centres of high-tech production. Some computer parts begin life in the US (often with female labour of Latin or Asian origin) and are then sent to the Third World for a middle production stage (again with female labour) before coming back to the US for final assembly. Even some clerical work is now being done in poor countries and sent back to the US on magnetic tape – the entire Third World part of this operation can cost less than the office space alone in the US. None the less, well-documented cases of long-term working with organic solvents leading to headaches, flu-like symptoms and nose bleeds do occur, and are almost certainly the tip of an unsavoury iceberg. One case at least led to the death of the victim.

One Malaysian government document remarks enticingly,

> The manual dexterity of the Oriental female is famous the world over. Her hands are small and she works fast … who could be better qualified by nature and inheritance to contribute to the efficiency of the bench assembly production line?

Robots, computers and society

The implications of the revolution are immense. Certainly, several million **jobs** will be created by this new industry. What is much less sure is whether the Luddites, who always feared that machines would create fundamental unemployment, have finally been vindicated. It may be that the connection between economic growth and employment has finally been broken.

Many governments (let alone corporations) around the world are investing heavily in high technology. They know that even if the long term effects will be huge increases in unemployment (or at least in employment as we understand it – see **Job**) in the short and medium term, any country which ignores computers and robots will be hopelessly outcompeted.

There is no avoiding the new technology – what will count is to survive somehow and flourish alongside it. As one American pundit put it, 'Automate, emigrate or evaporate.'

Joe Engelberger has been called the Father of the Robot. He founded Unimation Inc, the US robot firm wih plants in Britain, having read Isaac Asimov's I, *Robot* in 1942. He told *New Scientist* (24 Feb 1983) that

> We'll eventually have our robots, like Boston ladies have their hats. It will go slowly, that's the first thing to say. It won't happen overnight, so I don't think we should worry. I guess politicians are going to have to worry about productivity. Any country that does not increase its productivity will not continue to manufacture goods. Its people will end up being in servicing, they will not be manufacturers .... If you create this wealth, the big problem for government is distribution. We don't have a fair distribution system in the world, there's no question about it. The only way we know how to make the entire people do better is to bring up the whole schmear ... If we can create all this wealth, the problem is for the politicians to figure out ways to distribute it more equitably. If we don't, I guess that the visibility of poor people will be so clear, so painful, that we will have uprisings ... it's a great challenge.

29 Batteries: carrying, and dumping, clever chemistry

BATTERIES are an integral part of the convenience world, in which electrical goods of all kinds must be portable. But these small objects are replete with chemicals of every sort, all of which are toxic to some degree or other. The following is a list of some of the things you might find in the batteries you use, and therefore in the rubbish dumps to which they are consigned when their life is over:

zinc
mercuric chloride
lead
cadmium
methyl cellulose
ammonium chloride
zinc chloride
oxides of mercury
oxides of silver
oxides of manganese
oxides of copper

Around a quarter of a million tonnes of batteries are produced in the UK every year, using something like 120,000 tonnes of lead, zinc, cadmium and other metals, to produce tens of millions of cells. Car and heavy batteries dominate the total weight of batteries sold and scrap generated. Their lead scrap is mostly recovered pretty efficiently, but the metals of the remaining sorts of battery are often used for a month or two and then junked.

The junked batteries of the UK represent about 12,000 tonnes of lead, about the same amount of zinc, and about 300 tonnes of nickel, cadmium and mercury dumped into the environment. Almost all the zinc, mercury, cadmium, nickel and silver which gets wasted in the UK is wasted through having been made into batteries and then dispersed throughout the country in cells whose scrap value is nil.

The battery epitomises the chemical fall-out which is part and parcel of modern society, and whose impact we have been slow to assess. The effect of chemical pollution is the Cinderella of environmental concern. This is partly because toxic waste is such dangerous stuff, and so unattractive, that few people dare to investigate it; partly because it is so shrouded in commercial and state secrecy; and partly because its effects are so hard to quantify. Much of the evidence is circumstantial and anecdotal. These factors contribute to an anxiety amongst citizens which is hard for them to substantiate or act upon. Moreover, the worst fears of people living near dumps or downstream or downwind of plants do seem, rather often, to be justified.

The problem is not limited to the capitalist or the rich worlds. Industrial air pollution, indeed, is worse in communist countries where protest is stifled. Czechoslovakia and Poland, for instance, are suffering from heavy-metal pollution – notably mercury, lead and cadmium – dumped from the sky by the smokestacks of heavy industry. Polish vegetables were found to be routinely polluted by heavy metals. In general, the citizens in those countries have a harder time even than those in the West acquiring and using information against their governments and industries.

Waste, US style

US official agencies reckon that since 1960, something like 500 million tonnes of hazardous wastes have been dumped in the country's 100,000 industrial disposal sites.

The Swedes reckon that they generate around half a million tonnes of seriously hazardous chemical waste a year. The British don't compile statistics on the subject, but experts reckon that around 5 million tonnes of seriously hazardous wastes are generated in the UK every year, and it has been suggested that a further 3 or 4 millions tonnes of the stuff goes missing each year.

Of the 60,000 chemicals (made in 6,000 plants) on sale in the US, only 20% have been tested to even minimal safety requirements. A further 1,000 new chemicals join the list every year. Three quarters of a million firms in the US generate toxic waste.

Beyond the risk of contamination from careless or ignorant waste disposal, in a real sense we are each of us repositories of waste toxics. They turn up in our food, for instance, so that virtually all of us will contain in our cell tissue varying quantities of toxic chemicals, most of which were unknown to man a couple of generations ago.

Of course, people were contaminated by noxious chemicals in the past: fumes from factories, or poisonous substances such as mercury and lead, which were used very much more commonly and casually than now. What is odd is the way in which people are now alert to the dangers of chemicals, and yet most regulatory systems have allowed problem substances to be used until they are proved dangerous, rather than otherwise. Nor is regulation in step with our, so far very limited, understanding of the effects of

"What I sometimes feel like doing, is enclosing a little packet of waste material with every one of the products we sell, just to remind people that they can't have one without the other."

Chemical company waste disposal officer, quoted in *The Listener* 21 January 1982

new chemicals, which is bedevilled by their effects being very long term and their dosages often being very small. Moreover, we know even less about the effects of exposure to a cocktail of chemicals than about any one of the constituents alone.

The next wave of environmental awareness is likely to concentrate on cleaning up the chemical-use chain, ensuring that from manufacture, through application and to their hanging around as residues in our bodies or in the ground and water supplies, chemicals are policed far more carefully. The problem is that people's awareness of the dangers of chemicals is patchy, but dependence on them – if only for convenience – very insidious.

Horror stories abound in the toxic-waste world. The disasters of Love Canal and Times Beach in the US, and others around the world, where dioxin (a component of many weedkillers and a hideously powerful poison) was found to have contaminated communities, alerted people to the dangers of such chemicals. However, this awareness did not stop their routine application as ingredients in pesticides, although some applications were forbidden. It took the dioxin disaster at Seveso, northern Italy, in 1976 (and the subsequent sorry tale of the largely illicit disposal of the contaminated materials after the clean-up there) to heighten awareness of the problems of the chemical in Europe. The EEC tightened up some of its regulations in the wake of the tragedy.

There have been serious claims that the fertility of much American sperm is falling fast, and the blame is laid on the new chemicals we now encounter daily. The cancer epidemic is often attributed to the new substances we ingest so carelessly; a US citizen now has a one-in-three chance of developing cancer, and many of these cases will be younger than used to be expected.

"Almost half of the green (unroasted) coffee beans that are imported into this country and tested have been found to contain illegally high residues of pesticides that have been banned or greatly restricted in the United States because they cause cancer."

Lewis Regenstein, *Environment*, December 1983

Even after many dangerous chemicals (but by most accounts far too few) have been banned for pesticide use, much human breast **milk** in the rich world is reckoned to be so contaminated that it could not be sold in supermarkets on toxic-danger grounds. However, women can go some way towards cleaning up their diet by renouncing as much animal produce as possible, and by being choosy about their vegetable buying.

Banning chemicals in the rich world seldom prevents their use in the poor world, thus poisoning people there, and their re-entry into rich countries in imported food (see **Livestock** and **Jeans**). Meanwhile in one sample of produce bought in San Francisco by the Natural Resources Defence Council, 44% of the vegetables were found to contain traces of pesticides. And even buying food labelled as organic may not be the saving move: many of them would not pass the legal definitions of being chemical-free (the California Certified Organic Farmers – 1920 Maciel Avenue, Santa Cruz, CA 95092 – police their members thoroughly, however). Nor is it only food which contains dangerous chemicals: the art materials used in American schools are reportedly rich in chemical solvents which are well known to cause lung damage and nervous disorders.

Toxics in India (and West Virginia)

In late 1984, the central Indian city of Bhopal suffered the greatest chemical tragedy man has yet inflicted on himself. A minimum of 1,750 people died there. Thousands more suffered injuries whose effects may well endure for the rest of their lives, many of which will have been shortened as a result of faulty plant management at a pesticide plant part-owned by the American giant, Union Carbide. The firm was not best pleased when it transpired that the same killer gas, methyl isocyanate, had been leaked periodically over the years at its plant at Institute, West Virginia.

About 100,000 people die from pesticide-related disease every year in the developing world, where 20% of the world's pesticide, and especially the most dangerous kinds, are used. Many of them are imported from countries such as the US, a third of whose pesticide exporting is of chemicals banned for use at home. One of President Reagan's first acts on taking office was to quash a valuable reform in the rules governing US exports of dangerous chemicals to the Third World.

There is a good deal of anxiety that the Indian government, in its enthusiasm to produce rather than import its pesticides, had been lax in its treatment of safety aspects at Bhopal. Often, Third World countries are so anxious to obtain production facilities that they in effect vie with one another in the ease of their operating requirements, leading to corner-cutting in safety matters.

But such problems are not necessarily a question of the rich world companies' indifference to Third World safety. Some governments – India's included – insist on the involvement of indigenous staff, whose skill may be in question. Often safety requirements involve planning matters beyond the operating company's power. At Bhopal, for instance, a shanty town had built up near the plant, and it was there that the greatest suffering occurred.

By early 1985 it was emerging that Bhopal's plant had been entirely built by Indians (to American designs)and was entirely staffed by Indians. Moreover, Union Carbide's American inspectors had, in 1982, presented to its Indian partners a major list of defects in the running of the system, which the Indians claimed to have put right by 1984. However, nobody from Carbide, apparently, went back to check.

The Third World and the rich world's waste

There is an increasing emphasis on rich world countries exporting their problems. China has been considering storing nuclear waste from rich countries in its deserts. A US company has been reported as offering $25 million to Sierra Leone to take some of its hazardous mining wastes. Nigeria, Liberia, Senegal and Chile have all been looking to Haiti as a potential destination for their wastes. Mexico and the Dominican Republic are said to have taken hazardous waste.

Managing dangerous waste

With stories of chemical waste dumps and their dangers becoming notorious, some US chemical companies are reported to be in favour of setting up a privately run clean-up fund which would back up the government's own superfund. Already private waste management companies have been enjoying a boom in the States. The superfund is run by the Environmental Protection Agency, and funded by a clumsy system in which some rather well-behaved companies pay a disproportionate part of the private sector's share. The EPA's reputation has been rising in recent years, after President Reagan's early moves to weaken it backfired in scandals.

In Holland there have also been several major scandals, but the 1979 discovery that part of a new town called Lekkerkerk had been built over a dump containing 1,650 drums of chemical waste marks the beginning of the new awareness of the hazards of waste: 150,000 tonnes of earth had to be removed. East of Amsterdam an unsuspected dump of 10,000 drums containing, amongst much else, a good deal of dioxin, was soon found. In the ensuing investigations, 4,000 illegal chemical waste dumps were discovered in the country, and a superfund, US-style, was proposed.

Holland's disposal laws are tough. So tough that some of Holland's waste has been shipped to the UK, where a traditionally relaxed system has operated. The UK and the USA have shared the view that the best trick with chemical waste is to 'dilute and disperse' it. The Dutch and others have preferred to 'contain and treat' it.

There is speculation that the British government has been too easy-going with its waste disposal policies, and criticism in particular that each county should be left free to decide the degree to which it will accommodate its own locally produced waste. For the time being, a few sites – such as the notorious Pitsea in Essex – have to take a disproportionate amount of waste. They do not attempt to treat it, but instead allow it to sit for years, and gradually seep – apparently safely, so far – into the ground.

Fortunately, there may be quite rapid improvements in the technology of waste disposal: US scientists may have worked out a way of detoxifying one of the most hazardous chemicals, dioxin.

Burning issue

There have been so many scandals surrounding disposal of chemical waste by dumping it in the ground, that there has been interest in treating it to regain some of its value. So far, this has usually proved expensive, though increasingly firms are studying the idea of turning their product to profitable use, before allowing it to be called waste.

Waste is often burned in plants on shore. People living downwind of such places have accused them of causing various diseases. One plant in central

Scotland which disposed of plastic waste (in this case, including the notorious printed circuit boards) has been closed after a local campaign against it, though the company claims it was due to close anyway.

Avoiding the difficulties from land-based neighbours, some US waste disposal companies have turned to burning it at sea, which many environmental commentators have seen as a way of shifting, rather than solving, a problem.

Waste and water...at sea

The oceans have traditionally seemed a sensible place to throw unpleasant things away. The North Sea, for instance, receives about 11 million tonnes of sewage sludge every day, around 8 million tonnes of chemicals and heavy metals, and about half a million tonnes of oil. The Rhine washes 3,000 different substances down to the sea. The system is little controlled and little understood. We simply want to rely on the healing power of fresh salt water, and round the world we have been putting at risk all our ocean wastes, with problems especially obvious in relatively enclosed seas such as the Mediterranean.

Much of the waste in the North Sea arrives there from plants situated beside estuaries. On the Humber, for instance, there has been a long-running controversy about the discharge of acids associated with the production of titanium dioxide, used as a whitener in paint, and other products. Titanium dioxide plants have been the subject of a good deal of campaigning throughout northern Europe.

Waste and water...on land

One of the least understood problems is the chemical contamination of drinking water (see **Glass of Water**). Clean-water legislation in the US, for instance, surfaced in the 1970s and since; but it hardly deals with groundwater, from which drinking supplies are drawn. Perhaps a quarter of the people reliant on well water in the US drink from sources which have contamination levels which would ensure the closure of beaches where people swam. There are about half a million leaking underground petrol tanks in the US. It is reckoned that 20% of the nation's underground water supplies are polluted. Water for large-scale use is screened for 18 chemicals, but getting on for 130 chemicals are reckoned dangerous enough to be seriously worth screening for, and many small wells escape testing altogether.

In the UK, the attempts to clean up the clean-river legislation have been largely hijacked by industry, which has consistently and successfully argued against the introduction of firmer rules on industrial effluent discharged into Britain's dirty rivers, mostly on the grounds of loss of employment.

30 Condors: wilderness, zoos and big birds

THERE are somewhere between 3 and 10 million species of animal and plant life in the world; the higher figure has been given more credence since the extent of the insect kingdom's size and diversity has become clearer. We have recorded something like 1.5 million of these species. An average of about 1 animal species or subspecies is believed to have disappeared every year during the 350 years leading to the mid-twentieth century but now we may be losing 1 a year. More than half of the known animal extinctions which have taken place in the last 2,000 years have taken place in the past 80-odd years.

Extinctions matter as symbols of our tyranny over the planet. Although they are mostly caused by hunting and pollution (especially from pesticides – see **Jeans**) and habitat loss (see **Births**), we may depend on the diversity of species more than we think. We have found that wild strains of seed have sometimes rescued commercial crops whose health has been undermined by monoculture and the disease-spread it can encourage (see **Coffee**).

Increasingly science is finding ways of using natural products in health care. However, even beyond our functional need of wilderness and wildlife, it may be that simply spiritually they are more important to us than we appreciated. We may not realise the force of that argument until too late.

Staving off extinction

The California condor is a very rare bird, but it once could have been called the North American condor, its range was so extensive. Now its continued survival is a remote possibility rather than a probability. Its last refuge is so celebrated and limited that it is marked on US national road maps.

The bird can have a wingspan of 2.7m and a weight of around 11kg. In prehistory, its range stretched from Florida to Texas, north-eastern Mexico, Arizona and Baja California in the south, and up to British Columbia in the north-west, and possibly beyond all these points. It was extinct east of the Rockies by the time the Europeans began their push west, and bred only in

California by the turn of this century. By 1943, it seemed to be breeding only in a small mountain area in southern California. Then, the population appeared to be about 60 birds. Now the numbers are closer to 20 and perhaps less.

Enlightened Americans would like to save the California condors from extinction. The difficulty is that the only obvious ways of achieving their ambition would be to reverse the habits and tendencies of centuries. Instead they have felt they must choose other, more modern, methods.

Does the condor deserve extinction?

Condors are immense, rather gloomy-looking vulturine birds which live at the top of the world and the top of increasingly fragile food chains. They are soaring birds which live on dead animals. Few people can have seen one. The Andean condor which I have seen in London zoo is one of the saddest sights anywhere. It lives in a cage in which, though it can stretch its wings, it can only limp rather than fly or glide. London Zoo has been trying to breed from its various condors since the nineteenth century, and it was not until 1982 that a chick was born which survived. That chick will grow up into as useless and redundant a bird as its parents, though its ignorance of anything better may be an advantage to it.

Vultures everywhere are under threat from a modern shortage of dead farm and wild animals (the latter of which is a factor of the shortage of wilderness – see **Births**). In Spain there has been a programme setting up 'vulture restaurants' where carrion is made available to the birds. The sad truth for many of these creatures is simply that the sorts of herd animals on which they depended are no longer abundant or even extant.

The American condor, for instance, was a part of an ecological world which for thousands of years was changing in ways which did not suit it, but which has only recently so altered that the bird's survival was threatened. For instance, not until 100 years ago did the herds of bison in America become threatened. They had survived the pre-man world, and had done well even in the century or so when the Spaniards had equipped the indigenous Indian peoples with the notion of horse riding. But the white man's rifle and his nineteenth-century passion for astonishing numbers (whether in height of buildings or of hunting 'bags') did for them. The prairie herds diminished from something like 40 million in 1860 to virtual extinction by the 1890s: the most extraordinary species-cide known to man.

Other factors were against the condor. The ancient world in which they evolved was the age of the sabre-toothed tiger, mastodons and woolly mammoths; an age when there were fellow vultures with 4m wing spans. The Rancho La Brea tar pits on Wilshire Boulevard in metropolitan Los Angeles, 80km from the habitat of the present remnant condors, is a testimony to the fossil record they have left. But it seems that temperature

"We dispute in [the] schools whether, if it were possible for man to do so, it were lawful for him to destroy any one species of God's creatures, though it were but the species of toads and spiders, because this were taking away one link of God's chain, one note of his harmony."

John Bulwer, 1653, quoted in *Man and the Natural World* by Keith Thomas (Allen Lane, London, 1983)

181

changes saw off many of the ice-age animals which became extinct, and of which – in one sense - the California condor is merely the most tenacious survivor.

It may be that we should accept that this animal is simply one of the thousands whose capacity to survive post-ice age – let alone twentieth-century – life has now been tested to destruction. It may well be that even the most conservation-minded human society could not preserve the sort of vast range of country which would provide condors with the required privacy and diet. Many wild animal populations, especially those at the top of food chains, need to be very well provided with diet-animals, which in turn require large areas of wilderness. Populations of wild animals – condors are merely the most famous instance, but tigers are another – need to be extravagantly large if they are to preserve genetic health. It may be that we should mourn the demise of the condor respectfully, and even with a sort of reverence, but not with despair or with too much activity directed at preserving it artificially.

In other words, since man was not wholly to blame for its extinction, he need not be unduly guilty, or despairingly, probably uselessly active in trying to reverse the trend. Probably no possible or reasonable behaviour or undertaking by man can spare the condor from its fate. Not that everyone tries very hard. In 1984, a young Californian condor was poisoned by a lead-shot contaminated carcase it fed on. Hunters prefer lead shot, because it is cheap, although it endangers carrion feeders.

The difficulty now is how to preserve creatures whose requirement of wilderness is larger than we can expect to meet. The answer has, in general, been to take the wholly opposing route: to capture specimens and hope they will breed in.zoos. This is the 'hands on' policy, and it has attracted a good deal of controversy. It has already led to the death of 1 condor chick in California.

Doubly peculiar then that out of the controversy has arisen a limited 'hands on' policy for the condor in which over the past couple of years scientists have been trying to find a mate for Topa Topa, a 14-year-old Andean condor in Los Angeles zoo. A 10-week-old nestling has already been taken from its nest because it was being neglected and was considered to be at risk. In September 1983 the bird was apparently doing well, in its £230,000 condominium.

There is no evidence that a breeding programme will be successful. There are very many steps in the process and we know very little about any of them. They include finding a couple which will mate (and there actually need to be many couples); rearing the chicks to the point of release; reintroducing them to the wild (incredibly difficult); ensuring sufficient habitat; and perhaps providing 'vulture restaurants' for their continued survival. The amount of land required for a return to the wild of a few condors would be phenomenal.

Meanwhile, there is division between scientists who believe that we know

Opposite: does the condor deserve extinction?

too little about condors and that radio-telemetry could tell us more, if only scientists were allowed to attempt to trap and mark or plant transmitters on more birds. But then there are scientists who say that we know plenty about why condors are dying. 'They're being shot, eating poisoned carcasses, and running into power lines. We don't need radio to tell us that,' said one.

The conservationist Paul Ehrlich wrote to the US Fish and Wildlife Service in 1980:

> Even the most wildly successful captive breeding program would be for naught if there is not sufficient habitat to support the birds after re-release…The condor, therefore, should be preserved not just out of intrinsic interest, compassion and its own ecological role, but most importantly because it can serve as a rallying symbol for protecting large areas of habitat and thus many other endangered organisms.

Paul and Anne Ehrlich quote Kenneth Brower (the son of American Friends of the Earth boss, David Brower) defining the inner heart of the 'hands off' attitude, in *Not Man Apart* (the FOE journal):

> And what if nothing can bring the birds back? What if Gymnogyps, watching Los Angeles sprawl towards its last hills, has simply decided it is time to go? Perhaps feeding on ground squirrels, for a bird which once fed on mastodons, is too steep a fall from glory. If it is time for the condor to follow Teratornis, it should go unburdened by radio transmitters.

The California condor has become a symbol, perhaps inappropriately, of the American need for the wild and of man's final need to consider whether hunting, pesticides and building-land hunger are compatible with our need to leave some of the planet untouched by man.

Californian Condor

31 War: man's dark creation

IT would be preposterous to pretend to be able to count the cost of war. It is an activity so miserable, depraved, bizarre, yet quite often glorious and ennobling, and in any case occasionally morally unavoidable, that it passes understanding and defies accountancy, making attempts at them a kind of impertinence. However, it is worth at least looking at some tangible aspects of what war has wrought and might inflict on the earth, and also what preparedness for war has meant for modern people.

There are currently something like 18 million full-time soldiers in the armies of the world, and worldwide military expenditure in the 1980s is something like $650,000 million a year. Although this figure represents almost $150 per head of the world's population, it is especially grotesque since half of it is spent by the US ($400 per capita on defence) and the USSR.

In the rich world, around a sixth of the tax-take goes on the arms budget, though there are great discrepancies, with the oil-rich Arab states spending a very much higher percentage of government expenditure on defence than the rest. In developed countries such as the US and UK, governments spend 5 or 6 times more per capita on arms than on education. The UK spends a little more tax money per capita on defence than on health, but the US government spends almost twice as much on arms as on public health. The Netherlands, by contrast, spends well over twice as much on both education and health as on defence.

Worldwide, two and a half times as much money is spent on armed forces as on public health. The average individual in the 32 poorest countries of the world (leaving aside China and India) 'receives' more than twice as much defence expenditure as education expenditure, and 7 times as much as health expenditure.

Roughly speaking, 5%-6% of the world's gross planetary product goes on military expenditure, and, we can probably reckon, a rather higher proportion of resource depletion (especially of precious metals such as titanium) and of pollution (see **Batteries**). Much of this goes simply toward being prepared for war, let alone, of course, actually waging it.

There is a kind of normality to war. There was only 1 year in this century,

"If only I had known, I should have become a watchmaker."

Albert Einstein, on his making the nuclear bomb a possibility

1909, in which there was not a major war in progress somewhere in the world. We have been spared nuclear war, but on the remorseless logic of the use of military ingenuity in the past, and of fatalities caused by successive wars, we cannot but half expect that sooner or later this technology will be used in anger or error, as all others have been. Such a war might then add its statistics to the historical track record that man always uses his exponentially increasing destructiveness.

Nuclear destruction

If all the nuclear weapons in the US and USSR were deployed against the cities of the world, each could be destroyed 7 times over. In its assessment of nuclear war and its effects, the American Office of Technology Assessment reckoned that an attack on a single city such as Detroit or Leningrad with 1 large weapon or 10 small ones would probably cause up to 2 million immediate deaths and many more injuries, many of which would turn into fatalities. Moreover parts of the city would be very hard to rebuild. The long-term ecological effects were reckoned to be small. An all-out assault deploying a 'large fraction of existing arsenal' would result in up to 160 million immediate deaths and virtually incalculable injury, death and disruption in the short and long term.

The long-term effects of a large nuclear catastrophe on the world's ecological system threaten man's foodbase, possibly for many years and maybe irreparably. No one has the means to do more than the sketchiest guesstimates, but it is thought that the bombs' huge generation of heat might result in the transformation of thousands of tonnes of the atmosphere into various oxides of nitrogen, which might produce a smog effect of disastrous proportions – the 'nuclear winter' – whilst threatening the ozone layer and thus plant, animal and fish stocks.

Long-term radiation hazards are also impossible to compute, but it is reckoned that a single one-megaton groundburst would present a lethal dosage of nuclear radiation to all exposed animal forms over an area of about 36,000 hectares. A single 15-megaton blast 30 years ago deposited lethal fallout over an area approximately the size of Massachusetts and the test island concerned remains uninhabitable even now.

It has been reckoned by a report for the UN that if an East-West conflict in Europe should involve the use of 1,500 nuclear shells and 200 nuclear bombs by each side against military targets (this would amount to one sixth of NATO's stockpile of these weapons) there would be 5 or 6 million civilian casualties, half a million military casualties, and over 1 million longer-term radiation deaths. Rear Admiral Eugene Carroll, one time commander of NATO's nuclear forces, has said of this sort of prospect; 'You can destroy Europe this way, but you can't defend it.' A senior generation of NATO commanders have now renounced their previous belief that Europe can be

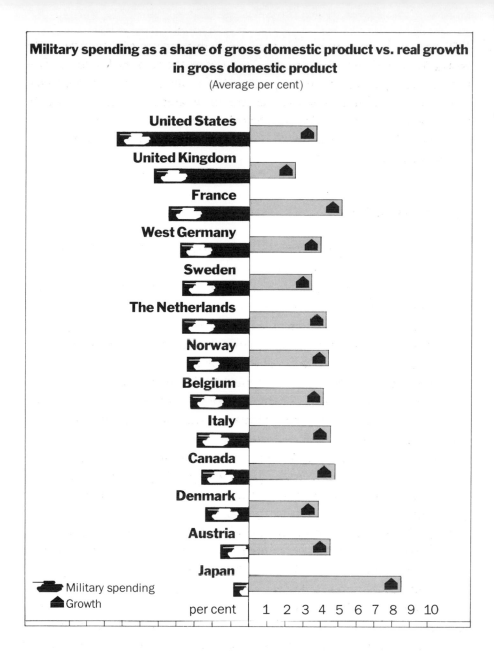

Military spending as a share of gross domestic product vs. real growth in gross domestic product
(Average per cent)

United States
United Kingdom
France
West Germany
Sweden
The Netherlands
Norway
Belgium
Italy
Canada
Denmark
Austria
Japan

Military spending
Growth

per cent   1 2 3 4 5 6 7 8 9 10

defended by nuclear deterrence. Many of them have been arguing for an increasingly 'conventional' but purely defensive posture being adopted by the West.

Conventional arms

Even conventional weapons are awesome, though modern defensive ones can be rendered increasingly accurate and 'pure' in their function against, say, invading tanks. It is estimated that 20 million lives have been lost worldwide in violent conflict since the Second World War. Britain has lost well over 3,000 servicemen in non-nuclear conflict in the 38 years of 'peace' since 1945 and over 1 million servicemen's lives in the two World Wars. The US lost 58,000 men in the Vietnam war, whose survivors have been largely unhonoured for their sacrifices. In Britain there remain 18,000 wounded men from the First World War and a quarter of a million from subsequent conflicts.

The conflict in Northern Ireland – whose tragic origins are so misunderstood around the world – has cost the lives of 500 UK servicemen since the late 1960s. But 13,000 people a year have emigrated from Northern Ireland in the course of the recent troubles, which is something like double the rate of emigration which had obtained previously. This is just one indication of how the troubles take their toll in family life.

The costs of war are likely to become yet more complicated to assess as we become increasingly able to wage ecological war. Herbicide spraying during the Vietnam war was undertaken under the code names Food Denial and Cover Denial. Much of the one eighth of South Vietnam which was sprayed will not grow food in the forseeable future. The US used 72 million litres of herbicides, including 44 million litres of Agent Orange, and the medical effects on people who came into contact with the chemicals, including liver cancers and birth defects, are an enormous problem.

Several thousand US ex-servicemen and their families have been pressing the Veterans Administration for pensions on the ground that they are suffering disorders as a result of handling Agent Orange, which contained the highly toxic dioxin, whose manufacturers are also being sued.

Bomb craters disfigure the South Vietnamese landscape, part of the result of dropping more conventional explosives on Vietnam than were employed during the Second World War.

Gas killed around 100,000 and wounded around 1.3 million people in the First World War, and there is no doubt that modern gases and other chemical warfare methods will be very much more powerful than anything seen then. The technology of chemical war grew mostly from pesticide research. At present, the US and USSR have considerable quantities of chemicals for war purposes, and France is believed to have quite a stockpile. Britain is believed to have destroyed hers in the 1950s and 1960s, but is linked into the chemical network supported by the Western allies, including the NATO countries and Australia. Britain does much of the fundamental research for the chemical warfare effort of the US, but says it undertakes no manufacture.

Whilst the Western world increasingly relies on nuclear weapons to deliver and counter terror, the wars which actually happen, rather than merely and hideously threaten, depend on conventional resources, which are, in spite of huge overall expenditures, squeezed financially. The British were able to re-invade the Falkland Islands in the first part of 1982, but it is unlikely that the operation could have been undertaken 2 or 3 years later: under plans then in existence many of the ships involved were due to be scrapped or sold. The British lost 243 men (excluding 12 civilians) and 777 men were wounded. The government spent about $2.3 billion on the

"... war has broken out ... a typical day: cool, overcast but dry, with a light breeze ... Someone launches a chemical attack ... using the nerve agent sarin ... The breeze causes the gas to drift: any unprotected person up to 25 kilometres away is killed. People twice this distance from the battle are seriously injured. There are millions of casualties."

Alastair Hay, lecturer in chemical pathology, *New Scientist* March 22 1984

conflict and its immediate aftermath. Fuel alone cost $345 million.

Does war control population?

We do not know where this fantastic state of military preparedness will lead in the future. For the recent past, ecologist Arthur Westing (see **Births**) has done some figures for what he calls high-fatality wars, especially those that took place within this century. By high fatality, he means those that claimed more than 30,000 dead. He reckons there have been 45 of these since the turn of the century, and that in total they claimed some 86 million lives.

Of those, 50 million were claimed by the Second World War alone, though during the period of that war – and in spite of its awesome toll – world population actually rose by 25 million humans. Around 1,600 million were living in 1900, and 4,700 were born during the next eight decades: about 1.4% of these suffered premature death in major wars, and perhaps a further 0.02% in 'minor' wars. Thus no war has yet diminished the world's population absolutely, but only served to slow its increase marginally.

Victims of war: refugees from fighting in the Chouf mountains, Lebanon.

189

Reading list

My interest in the environment and the wider implications of how we live really took something like adult form, I think, with reading Ivan Illich in the early 1970s. He is a writer one either loves or hates, and I confess to admiring his work vastly though of late it has become a trifle over-egged. I recommend *Energy and Equity* (Marion Boyars, London, 1974) as a starting point.

I can't read E. F. Schumacher, whose *Small is Beautiful* (Abacus, London, 1974) is so important an influence on many people. I have never tried to read *The Limits to Growth* by H. D. Meadows (Pan, London, 1974), which was the bible for a first wave of environmentalists. *Global 2000* (Government Printing Office, Washington, 1980) was a brave attempt to chronicle the potential damage we are doing the world, and some we may yet do. *The Resourceful Earth* by Julian Simon and Herman Kahn (Basil Blackwell, Oxford and NY, 1984) is a sturdy defence of our inventiveness and the earth's robustness.

One would not get far without the publications of *Friends of the Earth*, on both sides of the Atlantic. Tom Turner of *Not Man Apart*, FoE's US monthly, edits an elegant and informative paper. FoE UK has always produced useful campaign material, and continues to do so. Oxfam, the Worldwatch Institute (occasional papers and an annual *State of the World*, published by W. W. Norton, NY and London), and the Catholic Institute of International Relations (22 Coleman Fields, London N1 7AF, and c/o Africa Fund, 198 Broadway, New York, NY 10038) are all valuable sources. Perhaps especially so is Earthscan (10 Percy Street, London W1P 0DR and 1319 F Street NW, Washington DC 20004) which gets behind the overview syndrome to real cases in its regular paperbacks. *South* is an excellent UK magazine I see too seldom, and the *Economist* and *New Scientist* (UK) are essential. I found *The Times* and *Guardian* very clippable, and *The Listener* very rich.

I enjoy the UN Food and Agriculture Oganisation's *Trade Yearbook* and *Production Yearbook* very much (available from HMSO in UK, or Publications, FAO, 00100 Rome, Italy). The World Bank's *World Development Report* (Oxford University Press, annually since 1978) is invaluable. The Middle East Research and Information Project (PO Box 1247, New York, NY 10025) publishes good things, and the many commercial magazines on Africa are a rich vein. The US

Congress Office of Technology Assessment (Washington, DC, 20510) has published extraordinary data about environmental problems, and makes one wish the British had a similar bureau.

Environmental Management in Tropical Agriculture by Goodland, Watson and Ledec (Westview Press, 5500 Central Avenue, Boulder, Colorado 80301, USA, 1984) is full of information, as is the textbook, Human and Economic Geography, by Goh Cheng Leong and Gillian C. Morgan (Oxford University Press, 1982), whilst Ecology 2000 edited by Sir Edmund Hillary (Michael Joseph, London, 1984) is useful. The Cousteau Almanac by Jacques-Yves Cousteau and the Cousteau Society (Doubleday, NY, and Columbus, UK, 1981) is a vast but economical tome, which will soon need a new edition. Gerald Leach's Energy and Food Production (IPC Technical, London, 1976) is a classic study, and Food, Energy and Society by David and Marcia Pimentel (Edward Arnold, London, 1979) is a useful companion to it.

The Poor of the Earth by John Cole (Macmillan, London, 1976) was and remains a telling account of wealth and power in poor and rich countries. For a young person's guide to the issues, I suggest Charlie Pye-Smith's World Conservation (Macdonald, London, 1984). The enormous Atlas of Earth Resources (Mitchell Beazley, London, 1979) remains outstanding for its beauty, width of scope, range of concern and level-headedness.

Address list

Campaigners

Friends of the Earth, International Secretariat,
Box 17170, 1001 JD, Amsterdam, Netherlands

Friends of the Earth, UK: 377 City Road, London EC1

Friends of the Earth, USA: 1045 Sansome Street, San Francisco, CA 94111, USA

Greenpeace International, Temple House,
25 High Street, Lewes, East Sussex, BN7 2LU, UK

The Ethical Investment Research and Information Service,
266 Pentonville Road, London N1 9JY
UK campaign for shareholder responsibility.

Oxfam UK, 274 Banbury Road, Oxford, OX2 7DZ, UK
Oxfam America, 115 Broadway, Boston, MA 02116, USA

World Development Movement, Bedford Chambers, Covent Garden,
London, WC2E 8HA, UK

Intermediate Technology Development Group,
9 King Street, London WC2, UK

Intermediate Technology Development Group North America,
PO Box 337, Croton-on-Hudson, New York, NY 10520, USA

(Both these last promote appropriate technology around the world, along the
Small Is Beautiful lines promulgated by E. F. Schumacher (see **Reading List**).

Alternative trading organisations

Traidcraft PLC, Kingsway, Gateshead, NE11 0NE will send a wide-ranging
catalogue of Third World products for sale in UK. As best they can, they will also
answer specific enquiries about ATO's around the world, but please send $5 or
£3 to cover their administration costs in such queries.